So many in the body of Christ are walking around broken and bruised—bleeding on the inside—because they won't allow Jesus Christ, our healer, to touch the place that hurts the most. They've built walls. They've adapted to the pain. And now, that hurt is shaping their identity, their relationships, and their destiny. That's why I'm so grateful for *Healing Hurts* by Pastor Jonathan Miller.

This is more than a book—it's a divine invitation. Page after page, Pastor Miller brings biblical truth, heartfelt wisdom, and Spirit-led guidance to those who are ready to be made whole. He exposes the lie that time alone heals all wounds and reveals the only true source of healing: Jesus Christ.

If you're tired of managing your pain and ready to be truly free to live victoriously, this message is for you. *Healing Hurts* is timely, anointed, and urgently needed today. I recommend it wholeheartedly.

—Dr. Rod Parsley
Founding Pastor, World Harvest Church

Healing Hurts is a powerful and deeply personal book that speaks to the pain we all carry—and the healing we all desperately need. Born out of an eighteen-year journey through tragedy and trauma, this book offers more than just encouragement. It delivers practical tools and spiritual truth to help you process your pain and find lasting freedom.

In a world where we're taught to bury wounds and build walls, *Healing Hurts* tears those walls down with grace, wisdom, and timely insight. If you're ready to stop surviving and start truly living, this book will guide you from brokenness to breakthrough, from fear to freedom, and from pain to purpose.

This is more than a book—it's a road map to wholeness for you and the generations that follow.

—Ron Carpenter
Senior Pastor, Redemption Church

My friend Pastor Jonathan Miller has written a book filled to the brim with truth and healing

we wrestle with past hurts, grief, or deep wounds that seem, at times, just too much to bear. Hard seasons like this affect us all, and no one is immune. Whether you are dealing with emotional trauma, relational wounds, or even spiritual abuse, *Healing Hurts* will remind you that while the process may be challenging and sometimes difficult, God's love and healing power will always bring us through to wholeness and victory.

—APOSTLE JIM RALEY
LEAD PASTOR, CALVARY CHRISTIAN CENTER

Some books you read, and some you experience. *Healing Hurts* is an encounter with the healing heart of God! Pastor Jonathan Miller doesn't just write words on a page; he releases a prophetic invitation to step out of the shadows of pain and into the glorious light of healing and freedom.

—AARON AND AMANDA CRABB
PASTORS, RESTORING HOPE CHURCH

Whether you are seeking personal growth or desiring to impact future generations, this book offers a road map to a brighter, more abundant existence. Dive in and discover the transformative power of true healing today!

—BISHOP JOHN FRANCIS
SENIOR PASTOR, RUACH CITY CHURCH
INTERNATIONAL DIRECTOR, RUACH NETWORK OF CHURCHES

Healing Hurts is a powerful, transformative read that guides readers through the often painful yet necessary journey of personal growth and healing. I love how open and vulnerable Pastor Jonathan becomes as he paints a picture of every layer of healing. He teaches us that there is grief in healing and it's OK. It's so worth it. With profound insight and honesty he takes us through the raw, vulnerable process of confronting our wounds, showing how the most difficult moments in life can lead to the greatest forms of self-discovery and strength.

Whether you're navigating emotional struggles or seeking ways to better understand your own healing path, *Healing*

Hurts offers wisdom, compassion, and the encouragement needed to turn pain into a source of power. You truly can turn your scars into stars and allow your pain to become your pulpit.

—KIMBERLY "REAL TALK KIM" JONES
PASTOR, LIMITLESS CHURCH

It is impossible to get through life without pain. It's what we do with it that matters. Managing pain is one thing—being healed is an entirely different thing. Jonathan Miller knows something about pain and healing. I'm proud not only to endorse this book but also to recommend it. Read it now; thank me later. You're welcome.

—BISHOP MICHAEL PITTS
FOUNDING PASTOR, CORNERSTONE CHURCH
OVERSEER, CORNERSTONE GLOBAL NETWORK

Healing Hurts is a timely and transformative guide for anyone ready to stop hiding behind pain and start walking in healing. Jonathan Miller writes with pastoral wisdom and prophetic insight, offering practical tools and spiritual truths that lead to real freedom. This book will not only help you break free from the past but also empower you to shape a new legacy for generations to come.

—BISHOP WAYNE MALCOLM
MOTIVATIONAL TEACHER AND EXECUTIVE COACH KNOWN
AS THE BUSINESS BISHOP

Jonathan Miller's *Healing Hurts* is more than just a book—it's a deeply personal and transformative guide for anyone seeking healing from life's pains. Drawing from his own experiences of enduring trauma, Miller takes readers on a compelling journey through struggle, self-discovery, and, ultimately, restoration. His words are both honest and hopeful, acknowledging the depth of pain while providing a clear path toward emotional and spiritual renewal.

—BISHOP S. Y. YOUNGER
FOUNDER, THE RAMP CHURCH INTERNATIONAL AND
ONE WAY CHURCHES INTERNATIONAL

Betrayal feels like a stab in the back—one you're not sure you'll ever survive. (I know. I've been there.) But limping through life nursing old wounds is exhausting! If you've ever been hurt (and who hasn't?), *Healing Hurts* by Jonathan Miller is a must-read. It's a spiritual first aid kit packed with raw wisdom and an honest prescription for healing. Stop slapping emotional duct tape on your wounds—your breakthrough starts now!

—DAVID CRANK
LEAD PASTOR, FAITHCHURCH.COM

Healing Hurts is a powerful and compassionate guide for anyone navigating the complexities of emotional pain and trauma. With profound insight and practical wisdom, this book offers a safe and supportive space to confront, process, and heal from past wounds.

—MICHAEL BOADI NYAMEKYE, PHD
LEAD PASTOR, THE MAKER'S HOUSE

Every message from Jonathan Miller is always transformative. In his book, *Healing Hurts*, Jonathan gives divine strategies that will aid every reader in overcoming the obstacles that plague their journey. His transparency will not only encourage readers, but it will serve as an instrument for deliverance and freedom. Restoration and elevation are the guaranteed outcomes for those who absorb the wisdom and apply the principles that Miller shares in this work!

—MARCUS GILL
FOUNDER, MARCUS GILL INTERNATIONAL

"Yesterday will demand your yes today"—yes to healing, help, hope, forgiveness, faith, to become better and not bitter. Pastor Jonathan Miller pens from the pain of past hurts and uncontrollable personal circumstances to a trajectory of triumph through Christ Jesus. You will glean from the fields of experience; you shall overcome, spirit, soul, and body.

—TODD HOSKINS
PASTOR, REDEMPTION CHRISTIAN TABERNACLE

Via his new book, *Healing Hurts*, my friend Jonathan Miller leads us through a soul-searching journey that confronts the raw reality of pain with the redemptive truth of God's healing power. This book doesn't shy away from the hard places—it walks you through them with grace, compassion, and practical tools that bring lasting transformation. If you've ever felt stuck in cycles of bitterness, fear, or dysfunction, this book offers a clear and hopeful path forward.

With honesty and biblical insight *Healing Hurts* shows us that healing isn't just possible—it's essential. More than just providing personal restoration, this book equips you to break generational cycles and step boldly into your God-ordained future. It's a must-read for anyone ready to trade pain for purpose and live in the fullness of freedom.

—Tony Suarez
Founder, Revivalmakers Ministries

Healing Hurts is a timely and transformational resource for anyone ready to confront the silent pain that so often shapes our lives. With profound insight and practical wisdom my friend Jonathan Miller gently guides readers through the inner work of healing the heart, renewing the mind, and restoring the soul. This book doesn't just talk about change—it activates it. If you're tired of carrying yesterday's wounds into tomorrow's future, *Healing Hurts* offers the road map to freedom, wholeness, and generational change.

—Jeffrey Smith
Pastor, Strong Tower Church

Healing Hurts is a transformative guide for anyone ready to break free from the pain of the past and step into lasting wholeness. With compassion and clarity Jonathan Miller offers practical tools to dismantle emotional walls, overcome fear and bitterness, and embrace the healing power of God. If you're tired of masking your wounds and repeating destructive cycles,

this book will lead you to true freedom—empowering you to change your future and the future of those who follow.
—RONNIE JO HARRISON
PASTOR, THE KINGDOM CENTER

In *Healing Hurts*, Jonathan Miller masterfully moves readers from suppressed scars to supernatural strength. With pastoral precision and prophetic poignancy, he exposes the silent struggles so many carry and offers a clear, compassionate course toward healing. This book is not just a read—it's a recovery room for the soul. If you're ready to stop managing pain and start mastering freedom, then it may be providential that this book has found its way into your hands. This could just be the very road map that will guide you from trauma to transformation, not just for you but for the generations that follow.
—MIKE WHITE
SENIOR PASTOR, THE TAB CHURCH LONDON

Healing Hurts isn't just a book—it's an adventurous journey to emotional and spiritual wholeness. Using principles and revelatory truth from Scripture, my friend Jonathan Miller has given us a timeless manuscript to unlocking inner freedom. If you have ever suffered form hurt, trauma, or abuse, there's a good chance there are still some places in your life that still need healed. And I believe *Healing Hurts* is the necessary next step in your journey!
—BISHOP KEVIN WALLACE
LEAD PASTOR, REDEMPTION TO THE NATIONS CHURCH

HEALING HURTS

JONATHAN MILLER

CHARISMA
HOUSE

HEALING HURTS by Jonathan Miller
Published by Charisma House, an imprint of Charisma Media
1150 Greenwood Blvd., Lake Mary, Florida 32746

Copyright © 2025 by Jonathan Miller. All rights reserved.

Unless otherwise noted, all Scripture quotations are taken from the New King James Version®. Copyright © 1982 by Thomas Nelson. Used by permission. All rights reserved.

Scripture quotations marked AMP are from the Amplified® Bible (AMP), Copyright © 2015 by The Lockman Foundation. Used by permission. www.Lockman.org

Scripture quotations marked ESV are from The ESV® Bible (The Holy Bible, English Standard Version®), copyright © 2001 by Crossway, a publishing ministry of Good News Publishers. Used by permission. All rights reserved.

Scripture quotations marked MEV are from the Modern English Version. Copyright © 2014 by Military Bible Association. Used by permission. All rights reserved.

Scripture quotations marked NIV are taken from the Holy Bible, New International Version®, NIV®. Copyright © 1973, 1978, 1984, 2011 by Biblica, Inc.® Used by permission of Zondervan. All rights reserved worldwide. www.zondervan.com. The "NIV" and "New International Version" are trademarks registered in the United States Patent and Trademark Office by Biblica, Inc.®

Scripture quotations marked TLB are taken from *The Living Bible*, copyright © 1971 by Tyndale House Foundation. Used by permission of Tyndale House Publishers, Carol Stream, Illinois 60188. All rights reserved.

While the author has made every effort to provide accurate, up-to-date source information at the time of publication, statistics and other data are constantly updated. Neither the publisher nor the author assumes any responsibility for errors or for changes that occur after publication. Further, the publisher and author do not have any control over and do not assume any responsibility for third-party websites or their content.

For more resources like this, visit MyCharismaShop.com and the author's website at orlandonewbeginnings.com.

Cataloging-in-Publication Data is on file with the Library of Congress.
International Standard Book Number: 978-1-63641-483-6
E-book ISBN: 978-1-63641-484-3

1 2025
Printed in the United States of America

Most Charisma Media products are available at special quantity discounts for bulk purchase for sales promotions, premiums, fundraising, and educational needs. For details, call us at (407) 333-0600 or visit our website at charismamedia.com.

Portions of this book were previously published as *Healed to Minister*, ISBN 0-57801154-7, copyright © 2009.

The author has made every effort to provide accurate accounts of events, but he acknowledges that others may have different recollections of these events.

CONTENTS

Introduction 1

Chapter 1 Why People Do What They Do 7
Chapter 2 The What and the Why
           of the Matter 11
Chapter 3 Dealing with Iniquity 25
Chapter 4 The Problem 40
Chapter 5 Dysfunction or Destiny 47
Chapter 6 Messy Life, Messy People 63
Chapter 7 Irritation: A Part of the Process 73
Chapter 8 Stay Where You're Sent 86
Chapter 9 You Are Called to Lead 100
Chapter 10 The Process 105
Chapter 11 Surrendering to the Process 115
Chapter 12 Healing 125
Chapter 13 The Way We See 135
Chapter 14 Sabotage 153
Chapter 15 Relief or Cure? 164
Chapter 16 Get to the Root 173
Chapter 17 The Solution 187

Chapter 18 Getting Started 194

Chapter 19 A Closer Look at Forgiveness 212

    Conclusion................................ 231
    A Personal Invitation to Know Jesus 237
    Notes...................................... 239
    Acknowledgments........................... 241
    About the Author 243

INTRODUCTION

What if the worst day of your life became the start of something miraculous? Get ready—together, we are going on a journey. I will tell you upfront that the journey might be difficult and painful at times. It does hurt to heal, but I promise it will be worth it.

Along the way, I'll share with you the truths I learned—truths that were learned in one devastating moment that unraveled into an eighteen-year nightmare. Each one of these truths brought healing and freedom into my life, and I can't wait to unwrap them with you.

My journey began at twelve years old when my life, as I knew it, completely fell apart.

I'll never forget the day it happened. My father—my hero, my favorite pastor and preacher—confessed to my mother that he was unfaithful to her. The moment I heard the news, my heart shattered. I ran out of the house, tears streaming, wondering what would happen next.

Would my parents get a divorce, or would my mom forgive him? How would the church members respond? Would my dad be able to repent and be restored?

What would come of me? What would come of my family?

The following Sunday, I watched my father stand before our church and publicly confess his sin.

I saw people I had known my whole life—families who had spent weekends and holidays with mine—walk out of the church and out of our lives forever. Understandably, they were angry, shaken, disillusioned, and disappointed.

That was the day our church fell apart.

Yet, in all the chaos that followed, I saw my father find brokenness and true repentance. For the first time in his life, he found the courage to face whatever issues of dysfunction and insecurity had opened the door for his sin. He immediately checked himself into a Christian-based outpatient treatment center. Upon his release, my mother noticed the changes in his life. Just as quickly as tragedy struck, it felt like things might be turning around.

My mother agreed to attend extensive counseling with my father, facing their own personal issues, as well as addressing their relationship issues. During this difficult but healing process, my mother eventually made the decision to give their marriage a second chance. However, when her decision became public, things really began to unravel.

My father's infidelity opened a door to false accusations, leading to criminal charges being filed against him. It was another devastating shock. No crime had been committed. How could this happen? We were sure the truth would come out, that the charges would be dropped. But over the next year, our family found ourselves in court, fighting for our lives.

Introduction

Imagine our shock when, after a very lengthy public trial, my father was found guilty. He was sentenced to serve seven to twenty-seven years in a state penitentiary.

I can sum up the whirlwind of feelings I experienced upon hearing the news with two words: *utter devastation*. Just when it felt like we had a glimmer of hope, it was gone—just like that.

At the time, I was almost thirteen years old, and my father was ripped from my life—sent to prison for more years than I had even been alive.

I was afraid. I was confused. In the midst of even greater uncertainty, more questions arose. Would my mom stay married to my dad? Would she sell our home and leave town? Would I ever see my dad again?

Our church had dwindled down to nothing. Would the doors remain open? Nothing was certain—except for one thing. My heart was broken into millions of pieces. My life would never be the same.

When my dad was sent to prison, I was an eighth grader in a very small private Christian school. But the school closed down, and I was forced to attend a large public school. I had to grow up fast. I had to take care of myself. At the time of trying to survive a life crisis, I was experiencing all the changes and challenges that come along with being an adolescent.

To cope with the pain, I tried drugs and alcohol to help numb what I was feeling. Yet, through it all, I always felt close to God. I always prayed. I always worshipped. Oh, did I worship—hours upon hours of pouring tears out onto an altar. My heart was breaking, yet I was yielding to God's sovereign plan and purpose for my life. It was in those moments that I learned what true worship and complete dependency upon the Holy Spirit really is.

By the age of seventeen, I fully surrendered my life afresh to God. A few months later I was given the opportunity to preach my very first sermon. Immediately, doors began to open as I received invitations to minister in Indiana, Kentucky, Tennessee, Georgia, and Florida. I preached in small country churches, homes, barns, pretty much anywhere that would have me.

Growing into adulthood and becoming a minister of the gospel without my dad being present was difficult, but I still had things for which to be thankful. I'm beyond thankful that my mom not only stayed committed to their marriage but stayed equally committed to overturning his wrongful conviction and seeing his release from prison. I'm also thankful that we were able to visit him a couple of times a month. Those visits were painful. While I was always happy to see him, at the same time, it hurt to see him where he was. But most of all, it hurt when it came time to leave. (Much of what you will read in this book came through conversations around our prison visitation table.)

Now that I've told you about the mess, allow me to tell you about the miracle.

After eighteen years of wrongful imprisonment, my father received an executive clemency from the governor of the state where he was convicted.

In one day, in one moment, with one signature, eighteen years of impossibility came to an immediate end.

I will never forget the day my life fell apart.

But I will also never forget the day that God put it all back together again.

Introduction

On January 15, 2011, my father walked out of that prison and boarded a plane with me, my mother, my wife, and our first child.

He and my mother are still married today. And not just married—happily married.

Only God!

I want to show you what I learned "in the middle" of the mess becoming the miracle. I want to share with you that our character matters more than our gifts and talents. I want to show you that if you can have the courage to face not only the giants of dysfunction but also your fears and insecurities, you too can experience unimaginable healing and freedom. Healing takes courage. It hurts—but on the other side, there's abundant life. Are you ready to step into healing? Let's take that first step together.

Chapter 1

WHY PEOPLE DO WHAT THEY DO

Has a loved one, friend, coworker, or colleague shocked you by responding to a situation or event in a way that seemed totally out of character?

For example, imagine a colleague who is generally very kind and has become a good friend. You greet them on Monday morning with your usual "Hi! How are you doing today?" But instead of their normal friendly response, they snap, "How do you think I'm doing? I'm just living the dream over here!"

It catches you off guard. This isn't like them. Still, you assume they're having a bad morning. "Everyone has a bad day," you tell yourself, and you let it go. Then, before you know it, they stop talking to you altogether. Worse, they start spreading rumors behind your back.

Wow. What just happened? Stunned by the emotional ambush, you ask yourself, "What did I do? Why are they acting like that? Why did things suddenly change?"

More often than not, the answer comes down to one simple word: dysfunction.

Scenarios like this happen every day. Society has labeled this kind of behavior as *dysfunctional*. Oxford

Languages defines *dysfunctional* as "not operating normally or deviating from the norms of social behavior in a negative or unacceptable way."[1] The prefix *dys* means "abnormal," "bad," "difficult," or "impaired." So when you put "dys" in front of "function," you get "abnormal function," "bad function," "difficult function," or "impaired function."

Dysfunction affects much of human behavior. Dysfunctional people often come from dysfunctional families, forming dysfunctional relationships. And on and on the cycle goes. Simply put, when there's too much "dys" in front of the "function," people find themselves trapped—moving from one bad relationship to the next, from one unfortunate event to another.

I have the privilege of meeting and interacting with people from all walks of life, and I have yet to meet someone who didn't have a little "dys" attached to their "function"! If you think hard enough about it, I'm sure someone will come to mind. Perhaps you may even see your own face. But what causes dysfunction? What makes us do what we do? What caused your father to abuse you? Your mother to neglect you? A family member or person in authority to mishandle you? What made a friend turn on you without warning? Most likely *dysfunction*. We'll take a deeper dive into this later in the book.

DISCOVER YOUR DESTINY

Every person has a destiny and a purpose—including you! If you've surrendered your life to Jesus Christ, you have been called and anointed to minister Jesus to those

Why People Do What They Do

around you. But you cannot minister effectively if you are wounded, weary, and weak.

I once heard a prominent preacher say, "Ministry is born out of adversity." No one enjoys trials, but for many, adversity has been the pivotal point in their lives. Their destiny shifts from a matter of *chance* to a matter of *choice*.

One powerful example of this is Joni Eareckson Tada. In 1967, at just eighteen years old, Joni was paralyzed in a diving accident. Waking up as a quadriplegic seemed like a horrible nightmare. It just couldn't be real.

> IF YOU'VE SURRENDERED YOUR LIFE TO JESUS CHRIST, YOU HAVE BEEN CALLED AND ANOINTED TO MINISTER JESUS TO THOSE AROUND YOU.

As the days passed, her challenges became insurmountable. Anger held her captive.

Joni had a choice. Would she let pain hold her captive, or would she pursue freedom despite the tragedy? She chose freedom. That decision changed everything—not just for her, but for people around the world. Today, she is an acclaimed artist who paints by holding the paintbrush in her mouth. She is an international speaker and the founder of *Joni and Friends*, a ministry reaching people affected by adversity across the globe.[2]

Possibly, you've suffered some adversity in your own life. Maybe it wasn't physical adversity, like Joni's, but emotional adversity—rejection, abandonment, betrayal, abuse. No matter what form it takes, adversity leaves wounds. And unless those wounds are properly treated, they will become infected with unforgiveness, bitterness, anger, resentment, jealousy, hatred, and the inability to love and be loved.

If left untreated, those wounds will bind you to the adversity of your past, making it impossible to live fully in the present or pursue your dreams for the future. I've seen the enemy win this battle too many times, in too many lives. But my prayer is that as you read this book, the enemy will lose his grip over you.

> HEAL THE PAST, LIVE THE PRESENT, AND DREAM THE FUTURE.

It's time to heal. It's time to be free. Yes, healing hurts—but if you face the pain, you'll step into abundant life. Heal the past, live the present, and dream the future.

> The thief does not come except to steal, and to kill, and to destroy. I have come that they may have life, and that they may have it more abundantly.
> —JOHN 10:10

PRAYER

Lord, I'm ready! I am willing to take this journey even if it may not be comfortable. I am willing to face the pain so I can have abundant life. I thank You for the strength and courage needed to embrace this process. Adversity, betrayal, and abuse will no longer have power over me. I will be free of unforgiveness, bitterness, and anger in Jesus' name.

Chapter 2

THE WHAT AND THE WHY OF THE MATTER

P EOPLE HAVEN'T CHANGED much throughout history. We often focus on what someone does and miss the deeper question—*why* they did it.

To illustrate this, let's examine a fascinating biblical story involving David.

We think of David as the shepherd boy who killed a lion and a bear with his bare hands (1 Sam. 17:34–36). He's also the one who went into battle against the giant Goliath with just a sling and five smooth stones, emerging victorious (1 Sam. 17:49–50). His pathway was strewn with victories and accomplishments. Yet there came a time when he was involved in a love story gone bad—his marriage to Michal, Saul's daughter (1 Sam. 18:20–27).

A Love Story Gone Bad

The beautiful love story of David and Michal had a romantic beginning, but in the end, their relationship took a tragic turn. Michal, who once loved David, later despised him in her heart (2 Sam. 6:16). Their relationship, which started with deep affection, became a casualty of pride, resentment, and broken expectations. In the end, it became a love story gone bad.

The Bible tells us that Michal, the daughter of King Saul, loved David (1 Sam. 18:20). The details of how she fell in love aren't given, but it could have happened in a number of ways. Perhaps she saw him in the king's court one day while serving her father and thought, "Now that's a nice-looking man. I'd like to get to know him." Maybe she was drawn to his musical excellence as he played the harp (1 Sam. 16:23) or to his strength and character—along with the anointing on his life (1 Sam. 16:13). Regardless of what first captivated her, somewhere along the way, Michal fell madly in love with David.

Maybe you too have been bitten by the "love bug." Do you remember how it felt? That person is perfect in every way. You can't stop thinking about them. Suddenly, your whole life begins to revolve around them, and their presence changes everything.

When I started falling in love with Cristina (who later became my wife), my whole world shifted. My life revolved around her—what she wanted, what she liked, what concerned her. I made adjustments, fitting everything else around her because I was in love. After a beautiful courtship, we got married, and to this day my life still revolves around Cristina because I'm in love.

Michal probably felt the same way about David—so much so that she went to her father, eyes sparkling, heart racing, and said, "Dad, I've got to tell you something. I'm in love!"

The Bible says that Saul was pleased when he heard the news, and he immediately announced his intention to give Michal to David in marriage.

But why was Saul pleased?

Was he pleased because he wanted Michal to be happy? Or was it because he could use the marriage against David? The answer becomes clear in Saul's own words: "I will give her to him, that she may be a snare to him, and that the hand of the Philistines may be against him" (1 Sam. 18:21).

Saul's motives weren't pure. He didn't bless this marriage out of love for his daughter—he used her as a tool for manipulation. He saw an opportunity to set a trap for David, hoping it would lead to his downfall.

THREATENED BY SUCCESS

Saul hated David—especially after he triumphed over Goliath and the Philistines. This victory won David favor and respect among the people. When he returned from the battlefield, women poured into the streets to meet King Saul and celebrate the victory. They were singing and dancing jubilantly as they chanted, "Saul has slain his thousands, and David his ten thousands" (1 Sam. 18:7).

Instead of celebrating the victory, Saul seethed with jealousy. The women's song echoed in his mind. With every battle David won, Saul's hatred deepened. He wasn't just envious—he was afraid. And his fear fueled a deadly obsession.

Saul was determined not to let David take the throne. He kept a close eye on him, monitoring his every move. Scripture tells us, "Saul was afraid of David, because the LORD was with him, but had departed from Saul" (1 Sam. 18:12).

As David's reputation grew, Saul's hatred intensified. Yet David remained loyal, serving Saul with unwavering faithfulness—even as the king plotted his destruction.

On more than one occasion, Saul attempted to kill David. He even hurled a spear at him while he played the harp, trying to pin him against the wall. But David escaped: "And Saul cast the spear, for he said, 'I will pin David to the wall!' But David escaped his presence twice" (1 Sam. 18:11).

Saul's Desperate Plan

When his attempts to kill David failed, Saul devised another scheme. He placed David in a military leadership position, hoping he'd be killed in battle. Yet, despite Saul's efforts, David continued to serve faithfully, and his esteem among the people grew: "...all Israel and Judah loved David, because he went out and came in before them" (1 Sam. 18:16).

After repeated failed attempts on David's life, Michal revealed to her father the love that she had for David. This declaration of love gave King Saul an unexpected opportunity to launch yet another scheme to eliminate him.

According to custom, a dowry was required to marry a daughter. Saul knew David lacked the wealth necessary to marry into the royal family, so he devised an unusual request—one that would put David directly in harm's way with the Philistines, ensuring his death. To carry out his plan, Saul enlisted the help of his servants: "And Saul commanded his servants, 'Communicate with David secretly, and say, "Look, the king has delight in

The What and the Why of the Matter

you, and all his servants love you. Now therefore, become the king's son-in-law"'"' (1 Sam. 18:22).

To keep up his false pretense, Saul had his servants flatter David, praising his accomplishments and emphasizing how much the king and his servants admired him. Their goal? To convince David to accept the king's offer of marriage.

David's response must have startled them. Rather than welcoming their flattering words, he replied, "How can I, a poor man of little means, marry the king's daughter and become his son-in-law? I don't even have a satisfactory dowry to offer him in exchange for his daughter's marriage" (paraphrased from 1 Samuel 18:23).

The servants quickly returned to Saul and informed him of David's reservations. Because of his socioeconomic status, David did not feel worthy of the honor of marrying the king's daughter.

Saul sent his servants back to David with this message: "Tell David, as king, I don't desire any dowry for my daughter. All I require is one hundred foreskins of my enemies, the Philistines. That's all I want!" (paraphrased from 1 Samuel 18:25).

Saul hoped this unusual dowry would place David in danger, leading to his death at the hands of the Philistines, finally ridding Saul of him.

However, David eagerly accepted the king's terms. Wasting no time, he gathered his men, and together they slaughtered two hundred Philistines—twice the number required. Immediately, David returned and presented the foreskins to Saul. "Therefore David arose and went, he and his men, and killed two hundred men of the Philistines. And David brought their foreskins, and they gave them in full count to the king, that he might become the king's son-in-law. Then Saul gave him Michal his daughter as a wife" (1 Sam. 18:27).

With the king's request met and the dowry paid in full, Saul had no choice but to give his daughter, Michal, to David as agreed.

This arrangement pleased Saul, not because he thought David would make a good son-in-law, but because he saw Michal as a tool—a snare that could give him access to David and ultimately lead to his downfall. "Thus Saul saw and knew that the LORD was with David, and that Michal, Saul's daughter, loved him; and Saul was still more afraid of David. So Saul became David's enemy continually" (1 Sam. 18:28–29).

FOR BETTER, FOR WORSE

One night, when David came home, Michal pulled him aside. I imagine she said something like, "Hey, I heard a rumor today that my dad is sending messengers to kill you. There's no time to waste. If he succeeds, you won't be breathing by the morning" (paraphrased from 1 Samuel 19:11).

Michal felt compelled to warn David because she loved him. That love was evident in her willingness to protect him. It's true—when we love someone, we want what's best for them. Sometimes that loving concern even drives us to do things we never imagined.

That's exactly what happened to Michal. After careful consideration, she decided to help David escape by lowering him from the window. "So Michal let David down

The What and the Why of the Matter

through a window. And he went and fled and escaped" (1 Sam. 19:12).

When I picture Michal lowering David out of a window, something catches my attention. I'm sure you will agree—most people aren't strong enough or physically capable of doing such a thing. Being a king's daughter, Michal was likely delicate and graceful—it's hard to imagine her accomplishing this with ease. I believe that for Michal to do this, a supernatural strength must have been present. Her love for David was so strong that it enabled her to do something that, under normal circumstances, would have been impossible.

After securing David's escape, she moved into phase two of her plan. Based on the rumored death threats and the messengers her father threatened to send in the morning, she began preparing for their arrival. "And Michal took an image and laid it in the bed, put a cover of goats' hair for his head, and covered it with clothes" (1 Sam. 19:13).

To fool the messengers, Michal crafted a deception—using goat hair to fashion an image in bed that resembled David. When the messengers knocked on her door the next morning, she met them with a lie. "Uh, David is sick and unable to come out and talk to you" (paraphrased from 1 Samuel 19:14).

> HER LOVE FOR DAVID WAS SO STRONG THAT IT ENABLED HER TO DO SOMETHING THAT, UNDER NORMAL CIRCUMSTANCES, WOULD HAVE BEEN IMPOSSIBLE.

Because she loved David so much, she was willing to cover for him—even if it meant deceiving her father.

Saul's messengers left and returned to the king empty-handed.

No More Delays

The next day Saul ordered his messengers to return, demanding, "If he's still sick in bed, pick up the bed and bring him to me so I can kill him right in his sickbed!" (paraphrased from 1 Samuel 19:15).

Saul's messengers, now carrying out the king's direct orders, barged into David's residence and headed straight for the bed. Without hesitation, they pulled back the covers—only to find that Michal had deceived them. The bed linens held nothing but a motionless figure and a bunch of red goat's hair!

Furious and stunned, Saul confronted his daughter. "Why did you deceive me like this by helping my enemy escape?" (paraphrased from 1 Samuel 19:17).

Michal, caught in her deception, responded, "I didn't know what to do. I was afraid David would kill me if I didn't let him go" (paraphrased from 1 Samuel 19:17).

Here we see Michal's deep love for David that she would choose him over her own father. She risked everything—her safety, her loyalty, and even her relationship with Saul—to save David's life.

A New Plan of Action

Saul, furious over Michal's betrayal, decided to punish her for helping David escape. Because she was deeply in love with David, he gave her to another man named

The What and the Why of the Matter

"Palti the son of Laish, who was from Gallim" (1 Sam. 25:44), hoping to drive a wedge between Michal and David, putting an end to their romantic love story.

Determined to prevail over David, Saul launched numerous attacks against him, but David evaded capture each time. Eventually, after some time passed, Abner came to David, expressing his desire to make a covenant with him. As commander of Saul's army, Abner sought to join his forces with David's to help him overtake the throne.

> And David said, "Good, I will make a covenant with you. But one thing I require of you: you shall not see my face unless you first bring Michal, Saul's daughter, when you come to see my face." So David sent messengers to Ishbosheth, Saul's son, saying, "Give me my wife Michal, whom I betrothed to myself for a hundred foreskins of the Philistines."
>
> —2 SAMUEL 3:13–14

This was a strategic and sound military decision—giving David the manpower needed to become king over all of Israel. Yet David's actions revealed that Michal's return was even more important to him than securing the throne. "I'll make a covenant with you on one condition. You must first return my wife, Michal, to me" (paraphrased from 2 Samuel 3:13–14).

Though Abner agreed to the terms, he ultimately deceived David and did not return Michal.

RECOVERING ALL THE ENEMY HAD STOLEN

The Philistines launched a devastating attack on Israel, killing three of Saul's four sons—Jonathan, Abinadab, and Malchishua. Severely wounded in battle and unwilling to be taken captive, Saul fell on his own sword and died, leaving his son, Ishbosheth, to become the successor to the throne (1 Sam. 31:2–4).

After Saul's death, David remained determined to reclaim what had been stolen from him—including Michal. He sent messengers to Ishbosheth, demanding Michal's release from Palti. As David sought the Lord for direction, he was directed to go to Hebron and dwell there. "Then the men of Judah came, and there they anointed David king over the house of Judah" (2 Sam. 2:4).

David ruled in Hebron as king over the house of Judah for seven and a half years. Yet the prophetic word spoken over his life—that he would reign over all of Israel—was still unfolding. When Ishbosheth was later murdered by two men (2 Sam. 4), the elders of Israel gathered before David to fulfill what had long been foretold. "Therefore all the elders of Israel came to the king at Hebron, and King David made a covenant with them at Hebron before the LORD. And they anointed David king over Israel" (2 Sam. 5:3).

REUNITED AT LAST

Michal was eventually brought back after David was anointed king over the house of Judah, and the two were reunited. They were together again—restored, happy, and in love...or were they?

The What and the Why of the Matter

As David's story continues in Scripture, we see him experience both great military victories and painful defeats. The Philistines remained a constant threat, and as a warrior-king, David often led his men into battle himself. But it was in a moment of celebration, not war, that the tension between David and Michal would come to a head.

> So David and all the house of Israel brought up the ark of the LORD with shouting and with the sound of the trumpet. Now as the ark of the LORD came into the City of David, Michal, Saul's daughter, looked through a window and saw King David leaping and whirling before the LORD; and she despised him in her heart.
> —2 SAMUEL 6:15–16

Michal despised him in her heart! (That's a fancy way of saying she hated him.) But how? How could a love so passionate, so loyal, turn into such passionate hate? What changed?

Michal had once loved David enough to risk everything for him. She had lied for him, protected him, and even turned against her own father to save his life. So what could make love like that sour to the point of disdain and resentment?

THE ROOT OF BITTERNESS

Deuteronomy 5:9 speaks of the iniquity of the fathers being visited upon the children. I believe this holds the key to understanding the change in Michal's heart—her father's iniquity.

We will discuss this further in the following pages,

but first, let's look at the true source of Saul's hatred toward David—because it was more than jealousy, more than politics.

Saul's hatred of David went deeper than merely hating a man. He didn't just hate David—he hated God because God had chosen David.

Scripture, throughout the Old Testament, is very clear that God will visit the "iniquity of the fathers upon the children to the third and fourth generations of those who hate Me" (Deut. 5:9).

You see, Saul's hatred toward David was ultimately hatred toward God. And it seems that same spirit of bitterness that consumed Saul found a foothold in Michal's heart as well.

Where Did We Go Wrong?

Michal started out enamored with David. I'm sure, from her perspective, he could do no wrong. She saw a man of power, godly authority, and undeniable anointing—a man destined for greatness. She had to be smitten! From all accounts of Scripture, it's clear that David captured her heart.

One of David's greatest strengths was that he was a worshipper. He always had been! He was dancing long before the famous story in 2 Samuel 6. Even as a young shepherd boy tending his father's sheep, David had a dance, a harp, and a song. Worship wasn't just something he did—it was an integral part of his identity. And again, this must have been one of the things that first drew Michal to him.

But as time passed, the very things that once attracted

Michal to David began to repulse her. The qualities she once loved, admired, and respected became the things she resented and despised. Why? Because the sin of her father was passed down to her.

We begin to see this when Saul's cowardice and deceitfulness manifest in Michal. When she helped David escape and her father confronted her, she didn't boldly say, "Because I love him and I couldn't let you kill him." Instead, she lied, saying David had threatened to kill her if she didn't help him.

As the story progresses, we see Saul's hatred of David mirrored in Michal's hatred of David. I believe this happened for two key reasons:

Michal failed to confront the iniquity of her father. Her lack of self-awareness left her unguarded, allowing that same bitterness and deception to take root in her heart.

David failed as a husband and spiritual leader in his household to proactively address the generational iniquity Michal carried.

Sadly, this is often the case. We wait to deal with iniquities only after they manifest in destructive ways—but sometimes, by then, it's too late.

AS FOR ME AND MY HOUSE

Ask yourself: Am I willing to stand up and break the cycle? Will I take a stand and say, "As for me and my house, we will serve the LORD" (Josh. 24:15)?

This will not be permitted to be passed down to your children.

It stops with you.

It stops today!

Had Michal been willing to confront the generational iniquity of her father, things might have been very different. I can only imagine that maybe her growing hatred even took her by surprise.

Have you ever found yourself bitter toward someone without even realizing how you got there?

Perhaps, like Michal, you once loved someone deeply—romantically or as a close friend. Then, before you knew it, your love and admiration turned to bitterness and offense. You're left wondering, What happened? How did I get this way?

> **WILL YOU TAKE A STAND AND SAY, "AS FOR ME AND MY HOUSE, WE WILL SERVE THE LORD" (JOSH. 24:15)?**

It's possible that iniquity played a significant role.

PRAYER

Father, thank You for helping me identify my what and my why. Not only am I willing to acknowledge that some things have gone wrong, but I am open to You revealing why they have gone wrong. Reveal to me any iniquity, bitterness, dysfunction, or any other chain that may be holding me back. I am ready to be free. I claim that freedom today, in Jesus' name!

Chapter 3

DEALING WITH INIQUITY

INIQUITIES ARE DEEP-ROOTED weaknesses or tendencies passed down through generations. They often stem from parents or other family members, shaping behavioral patterns and ways of thinking that keep us trapped in our family mess.

Unless confronted and broken through the power of the Holy Spirit, iniquities will continue to be handed down, leaving generation from generation bound by the same struggles. Thus, the name "generational iniquities" was born.

Iniquities are frequently the driving force behind our behaviors and choices, often influencing us more than we realize. So let's examine this issue more closely and discover how to identify, confront, and break free from it.

The Conflict

In the previous chapter, we saw how the love story between David and Michal went terribly wrong. One moment, David was fighting for his wife, willing to forfeit a powerful league with Abner just to get Michal back. All his attention and energy were fixed on her.

Their love story seemed to be one filled with devotion and loyalty. Yet, just like that, "for better" turned to "for worse." And the next thing you know, the wife who once loved him so dearly was mocking him for the very things that once captured her heart. Again, I believe her hatred and disdain toward David flourished because she never proactively dealt with the sin and iniquity of her father.

FACING OFFENSES AND FAILURES

Think about the people you know who were once on fire for God—the ones who committed their lives to Christ, got plugged into a good church, and were all-in for God, now suddenly missing in action. They were faithful in every way. They served in ministry, volunteered frequently, and hardly ever missed a service. But then something changed.

> INIQUITIES ARE FREQUENTLY THE DRIVING FORCE BEHIND OUR BEHAVIORS AND CHOICES, OFTEN INFLUENCING US MORE THAN WE REALIZE.

One Sunday morning, you notice their usual seat is empty. You think, "That's odd." After church, you give them a call to let them know how much they were missed. They answer with what sounds like a perfectly reasonable explanation for their absence, stating things like "My child was sick," "I overslept," or "I just had a long weekend." You think nothing of it. Life happens, right?

But then the next Sunday comes, and again you notice

they're not there. You call again, and once more you are offered another string of excuses.

Then comes week three. Another Sunday. Another absence. This time when you reach out, they drop the bomb. "We're not going to church anymore."

Their words come as such a surprise. It's hard to believe what they've just said. Just a few weeks ago, they seemed to love being in church. They were excited, engaged, and part of everything. What happened?

Offense happened.

Somewhere along the way, offense crept in and took root. Maybe it was a pastor who unknowingly said something that rubbed them the wrong way. Maybe it was a connect group leader, a well-meaning usher, or a kids' ministry worker who unintentionally hurt them. Whether valid or invalid, the offense settled in.

And now? The church they once loved, they despise. The people they once served alongside, they now avoid.

But instead of focusing solely on what happened, let's go deeper. Let's ask the real question—why?

Not What but Why!

Many times, when people experience church hurt or offense, there is a legitimate reason behind it. In other words, the offense is justifiable.

However, I've seen time and again that not all church hurt is as it seems.

In many cases, undealt-with iniquities cause people to become easily offended. This is not to minimize the very real emotions the person feels but to acknowledge that many tend to see a problem when there really isn't one. They find themselves constantly questioning what people say, analyzing their actions, and doubting their motives. They see everything through a cynical lens—and the result is heartbreaking.

Their relationships with pastors, friends, and church family are sabotaged.

Consumed by bitterness, they leave the wrong way—only to repeat the cycle somewhere else.

So what is the wrong way to leave a church? It's leaving angry, bitter, with unresolved issues that cause your offense to spill over to others. Now what's the right way? First, it's important to know that it's OK to be hurt or even angry. It's OK to feel like your season at one church is over as you seek to find your next. However, it is important that your exit be honorable and that you don't allow your personal hurt or offense to influence or negatively affect others.

These seeds of iniquity may have been passed from their father, their mother, or past wounds. This is the real issue. This is *why* they did *what* they did.

We see this clearly in Michal's story.

Her problem wasn't just *what* she did—she didn't suddenly become jealous, stop loving David, and begin mocking him out of nowhere.

Something deeper is at play. The real question is *why* she acted the way she did. And the answer? The iniquity passed down to her from her father, Saul.

Now let's turn the question inward. What is in you that has set you up for sabotage and failure? Let's look beyond the surface and examine the why behind what people do.

Perhaps you've heard (or said) something like this:

- "I keep going from marriage to marriage." After the third one, my friend, it's time to ask why.

- "I don't know what it is, but every church I go to, I get plugged in...then I get hurt and leave." Let's find out the why of the matter so that you can finally be planted and flourish!

- "It seems like every relationship I begin starts out well, but it always ends with me being hurt and alone." Isn't it time to examine why this cycle keeps repeating itself?

Looking for the Answer

At some level, we have all felt the pain of sabotaged relationships. Whether we realize it or not, we set ourselves up for rejection. We set ourselves up for failure.

For example, ladies, maybe you find yourself drawn to lazy, unmotivated men—the kind who aren't ever going to do you any good. Or, men, maybe you keep getting involved with women who are extremely controlling and manipulative. You know you shouldn't be with them. You know they're toxic. But something in you keeps pulling you toward them anyway.

Why?

Because the iniquity within you is like a magnet, drawing you to the iniquity within them. Dysfunction attracts dysfunction. And before you know it—without even understanding why—you're on failed marriage number three, you're starting engagement number two, and you're attending your seventeenth church with your seventeenth pastor, wondering why people keep treating you the way they do.

What is it in you that has set you up for sabotage and failure?

There must come a point when we stop blaming everyone else for our condition and take responsibility for the iniquities in our lives that we have yet to address. I pray that as you've been reading the story of David and Michal, you've realized how different things could have been—if only Michal repented to David. Their story could have taken a completely different direction had she been willing to recognize and uproot those iniquities. Because make no mistake—iniquity doesn't just sabotage your relationships with people. It sabotages your relationship with God. "But your iniquities have separated you from your God; and your sins have hidden His face from you, so that He will not hear" (Isa. 59:2).

Stop Going Through the Motions and Start "Dealing"!

Over the years, I've seen so many people go to church and jubilantly express their love for God. I see them dance and shout. I see their hands raised, tears streaming down their faces. On the outside, their relationship with God looks strong. But too many times, these same Christians—so expressive in worship—are still battling internal strongholds of dysfunction and undealt-with pain.

Look, you can praise God as loudly as you want. You can show up to church every time the doors are open.

But if you're not dealing with the inside stuff, it's only a matter of time before you find your life in sabotage once again.

What iniquity have you invited into your life?

And before you start pointing fingers—please stop. It's not time to blame your husband or your wife. It's not time to blame your parents or your pastor. It is time for you to take personal responsibility. "Each one shall bear his own load" (Gal. 6:5).

What is it in you that has been allowed to control your behaviors, attitudes, and decisions? What iniquity have you invited in by readily opening the door?

This is total speculation, but if I were Michal, I think I would have wondered why David allowed me to be given away to another man—especially after I saved his life. Is it possible she was hurt that he didn't come and rescue her sooner? I don't know the answer to that question, but I do know this: Something happened along the way, and she opened the door for the iniquity of her family to sabotage her relationship with David.

BECOMING WHAT YOU HATE

People in sabotaged relationships often become the very thing they hate—and they don't even know why.

You see it in alcoholic homes. Children who grew up with an alcoholic father—who saw firsthand the pain, abuse, and negligence caused by alcohol's influence—often become alcoholics themselves. It's a hard thing to wrap our minds around. How can something that caused so much pain take hold in their own lives?

Because the iniquity and the hurt attached to it were never dealt with.

The pain turned to unforgiveness, and that unforgiveness opened the door for the iniquity to take root in their life.

When iniquity is not dealt with, a person is likely to become the very thing they hate. The very thing a person hates, they become because iniquity was never dealt with. "For what I am doing, I do not understand. For what I will to do, that I do not practice; but what I hate, that I do" (Rom. 7:15).

Angry, abusive parents often produce angry, abusive children—children who grow up and become angry, abusive parents themselves. Some are still bleeding from the wounds of their father's words, and that pain is then vented on their own children because they never healed. Others carry the deep scars of a mother's neglect—her lack of affection, her inability to nurture and love—and yet they end up infecting their own children with the same wounds.

It may not look the same. It may be disguised as something completely different. But at its core, the iniquity ends up doing the same damage.

You may ask, "Why?" Because it's a biblical principle. "The LORD is longsuffering and abundant in mercy, forgiving iniquity and transgression; but He by no means clears the guilty, visiting the iniquity of the fathers on the children to the third and fourth generation" (Num. 14:18).

The iniquities of the fathers (or the family) are passed down from generation to generation and become driving forces behind our actions, attitudes, and behaviors.

There's Hope

Now I offer you this hope found in Deuteronomy 5:10: "...but showing mercy to thousands, to those who love Me and keep My commandments."

Mercy is only activated through repentance.

Some teach that one prayer—a "once-and-for-all" prayer—is all it takes, and the moment you say, "Amen," you're free to do as you please. Well, in my opinion, it doesn't work like that.

Yes, the work of the cross is already done. But you cannot make a withdrawal from the eternal bank of God's grace and mercy without repentance. And repentance begins deep within the heart.

Grace is readily available because of the finished work of the cross, but you cannot make a withdrawal from that heavenly account without repentance. No one gets delivered without repentance.

> **GRACE IS READILY AVAILABLE BECAUSE OF THE FINISHED WORK OF THE CROSS, BUT YOU CANNOT MAKE A WITHDRAWAL FROM THAT HEAVENLY ACCOUNT WITHOUT REPENTANCE.**

Mercy and grace do not become activated until the Lord hears the words, "I repent."

You don't need mercy if you haven't done anything wrong. You don't need grace if you're not in trouble. But when we stand before God and say, "Lord, I repent for what I have done and for what I have become," something marvelous happens.

We are liberated. We are set free!

A Two-Way Street Called Mercy

Mercy is simply releasing (or forgiving) punishment where it is due. "Blessed are the merciful, for they shall obtain mercy" (Matt. 5:7). Mercy is a two-way street. It's something that we receive, but in return, it must also be given. So, when you receive mercy through repentance, the only right response is to extend mercy to those who have wounded you. When you release mercy upon those who have offended, betrayed, or hurt you, you are operating in forgiveness.

And here's a real secret: When you operate in forgiveness, you close the door to unforgiveness—which means you also shut the entryway for generational iniquities to take root in your life. They will still come knocking, but when you choose forgiveness, they can't come in.

Yes, mercy is something that is received, but in return, it must be something that's also given.

I've seen iniquity destroy many good men and women. I've watched it take down good husbands and fathers, good wives and mothers. Undealt-with generational iniquity will eventually deal with you. There is no escape.

Like cancer or another terminal disease, iniquity starts small—so small it may go undetected. But if it's not dealt with, it will inevitably come to the surface and wreak havoc. And ultimately? It will take you out and cost you your life.

FACE THE MUSIC

In my opinion, some Christians suffer from "head-in-a-posthole" syndrome—if I can't see it, it's not there. Most of us are reactionary by nature, avoiding confrontation as much as possible. We refuse to deal with our child's rebellion until it becomes so severe that drastic measures must be taken. We ignore the lack of communication in our marriage until the "D" word (*divorce*) is dropped.

But if we had addressed the issue beforehand, the "D" word never would have had a chance to be uttered.

We need to face the music and take action by being proactive rather than waiting until we're forced to react to a crisis.

Before my wife and I had children, we made a conscious decision to be proactive. Long before our two girls were born, we began praying against specific iniquities in their lives. Whenever either of us identified dysfunction in our families, we'd pause and declare, "We bind that and rebuke it from our children right now."

We were intentional. We were proactive. And we were shaping their future before it even began.

YOU CAN'T START TOO SOON

This process of identifying our family iniquities began before we even got married. As we started examining the iniquity present in our own lives, my parents played a key role in helping us navigate it. Because of their own healing and recovery, they had much wisdom and insight to share—despite the fact that their lives had completely fallen apart due to their dysfunction. What they learned in their healing process became a lifeline for us.

My parents would often give us premarital advice and counseling, and I can still remember many of those sessions—especially with my mother. I didn't like it. I squirmed in my seat, counting the moments until it was Cristina's turn! But deep down, I knew that every uncomfortable second I endured meant one less battle to fight in our future.

I'm so thankful that before our marriage, Cristina and I were willing to have those hard, uncomfortable conversations. We confronted and uprooted so many things before they ever had a chance to take root and become real issues. Even now, those same iniquities try to raise their ugly heads, but because we have been walking in victory for so long, we quickly put them back under our feet where they belong.

To this day, we approach our parenting in the same proactive way. Over the years, as we've corrected our children, we've made it very clear to them whenever we recognize the presence of an iniquity. We don't ignore it. We talk about it, deal with it, and refuse to let it take root in our household.

Because we know this truth: If we don't deal with it, it will deal with us.

It's never too soon to start *dealing*.

Dealing with Your Stuff

Have you sabotaged your relationships? Perhaps you've found yourself in one abusive relationship after another, one co-dependent relationship after another, one unhealthy relationship after another.

What happened? What changed?

What iniquity, what sin, did you give place to that caused your relationships to be sabotaged, your life to be sabotaged, even your relationship with God to be sabotaged?

You can deal with your stuff just as I did—and continue to do—and you can start right now!

Maybe your struggle isn't relationships. Maybe you sabotage your finances. Every time you start to prosper at your job or in your business, for whatever reason, you make a decision that throws you back into another financial mess. Debt pulls you back in. Your progress is short-lived, and just like that, you've taken thirty steps backward.

There's sabotage in your life—and it's because there's iniquity, a weakness, a character flaw that's been passed down to you. It has not yet been dealt with. But the Lord will show mercy if you release it through repentance.

Maybe you need to forgive your mother, your father, or your grandparents for the negative words they spoke over you. Maybe there's a deep healing and deliverance that needs to take place in your heart.

How desperate are you to be free?

How much do you want to be liberated from the cycle of self-destruction? Are you tired of being an angry, bitter person? How desperately do you want to be delivered from being that kind of mother, that kind of father, that kind of husband, or that kind of wife?

How badly do you want to be free?

According to Scripture, iniquity is such a serious

matter to God that He smote the womb of Michal, and she never was able to have children (2 Sam. 6:23). Symbolically, this speaks to us of the barrenness that comes because of not dealing with iniquity.

How many Christians are not living a fruitful life because they're offended, because they're hurt, because someone else's sin became theirs, and someone else's offense became theirs? Yes, they come to church every week with a smile on their face, but they aren't producing fruit. Too many are barren like Michal—incapable of bearing fruit because of the iniquity attached to their heart.

I don't know about you, but I believe I have been put on this earth for one reason: to bear fruit.

It's not to be a pastor; it's not just to be a husband.

I am called to bear fruit in every area of my life—my ministry, my marriage, my relationships, my job, my finances, and beyond.

And your purpose is the same: to bear fruit in whatever you do.

Don't let iniquity sabotage your destiny. Don't let it distract you from God's divine purpose for your life. The moment you surrendered your heart to Jesus Christ, your purpose shifted. You became part of His sheepfold—and sheep are meant to bear sheep.

From the very beginning, God gave this command: "Be fruitful and multiply" (Gen. 1:28). This was His first instruction to Adam and Eve. After the flood, He gave the same command to Noah: "Be fruitful and multiply" (Gen. 9:1).

Multiplication is essential for the expansion of God's kingdom. I want to be fruitful, and I don't want anything

Dealing with Iniquity

to stop me from fulfilling that purpose. I don't want hindrances, sabotage, or distractions to come between me and my King, my wife, my family, or God's people.

Oh, that we would all experience true freedom in fulfilling this purpose!

You can be set free from iniquity. Its driving force can be broken. All you need to do is repent, and as it says in Psalm 78:38, "But He, being full of compassion, forgave their iniquity..."

Today can be the first day of a brand-new life.

PRAYER

Father, prepare my heart for what You're going to do in my life.

Forgive me, Lord, for any place where I've allowed iniquity to reside in my heart. Lord, forgive any unforgiveness or bitterness I have allowed to gain entrance into my life. Whether it comes from my natural father, my mother, a family member, a grandparent, an aunt, or an uncle—Lord, I release it to You.

Forgive me for allowing hurts from past relationships to close me off, to make me an angry and guarded person. Today, I choose to close the door to that hurt.

Let freedom be released like a mighty river in my life.

Heal me, Father, that I may walk in wholeness, free from dysfunction, a healthy, restored individual moving in the fullness of my destiny and purpose. Amen.

Chapter 4

THE PROBLEM

What comes to mind when you hear the word *leader*? Do you think of extraordinary talent, a genius mind, or something else? Do you believe that great leaders are simply "born leaders"?

The legendary Green Bay Packers coach Vince Lombardi, one of the greatest leaders of all time, once said, "Leaders aren't born; they are made. They are made by hard effort, which is the price which all of us must pay to achieve any goal that is worthwhile."[1]

> "Real leaders are ordinary people with extraordinary determination!"

When you study history's great leaders, one truth stands out. The statement by an unknown author simplifies it perfectly: "Real leaders are ordinary people with extraordinary determination!"[2]

Individuals who distinguish themselves as leaders are rare and hard to find. Success as a leader isn't accidental—it is forged in the fire of life's most difficult battles. The person who is "born to lead" is one who chooses to grow through each battle, using every victory as a building block rather than a trophy, realizing destiny is a matter of choice, not a matter of chance.

NAAMAN, THE CAPTAIN OF THE HOST

> Now Naaman, commander of the army of the king of Syria, was a great and honorable man in the eyes of his master, because by him the LORD had given victory to Syria. He was also a mighty man of valor, but a leper...
> —2 KINGS 5:1

In Scripture, Naaman was recognized as a great leader. As the military commander of the army of the king of Syria, he was a man of prominence—essentially, in contemporary terms, commander-in-chief.

A mighty man of valor (2 Kings 5:1), Naaman had likely worked his way up from a lower rank, proving himself through battle, strategy, and leadership. His military prowess set him apart, earning him the highest promotion—captain of the host of the army of Syria. His ability to lead men into battle and subdue the nation's enemies made him a respected and trusted warrior.

Under Naaman's leadership, Syria became the dominant nation of its time. His military expertise was widely recognized, and he was regarded by all as an honorable man—"because by him the LORD had given victory to Syria" (2 Kings 5:1). His soldiers and servants highly esteemed him. His life was marked with victory and valor.

Yet, though he was recognized as "a mighty man of valor," Scripture interjects with a single sobering word: "But..."

"he was a leper."

But He Was a Leper

The word *but* is such a simple word—one we use all the time without thinking about how much this three-letter word changes everything. In this context, everything that comes before it is minimized.

What is your *but*?

She is pretty, *but* her attitude...He is a good guy, *but* he drinks too much...

"He was also a mighty man of valor, but a leper..." (2 Kings 5:1).

Let's examine Naaman's *but*.

I'm sure the moment Naaman became leprous, it seemed as if all his previous accomplishments became meaningless. Leprosy was one of the most loathsome, humiliating disorders a person could endure. To understand just how devastating this disease was, let's take a closer look at its impact.

In Naaman's time, leprosy was incurable and tragic. Its slow, almost insidious onset made it particularly cruel—easy to overlook at first, but impossible to ignore as it progressed. What started as small, unnoticed spots eventually led to severe physical deterioration. But it wasn't just the disease itself that tormented its victims—it was the profound social isolation that came with it. Banished from society, cut off from family and community, lepers endured both the physical ravages of the disease and the emotional toll of separation from loved ones and society.

Imagine Naaman's fear and uncertainty at the magnitude of his situation. At the pinnacle of his military career, he was marked for greatness, celebrated as a commander and mighty man of valor—*but* he was a leper.

How could a tiny reddish spot bring such a powerful leader to his knees?

Naaman was an honorable, victorious leader—a man who had risen to prominence and greatness, highly respected by all. How could one small blemish on his skin hold the power to change everything? Life was wonderful. His career was soaring. Yet, without warning, everything shifted when a little red spot appeared on his skin and began to spread (Num. 12:10).

Suddenly, he had a big problem—he was a leper.

Captain or Outcast?

Scripture doesn't tell us exactly when Naaman contracted leprosy, but we do know this—one of the most devastating consequences of leprosy was isolation. The moment a person was declared leprous, they were separated out from society, forced to live in loneliness and shame.

Now, imagine a great leader, a man of power and authority, suddenly cast out from the very people he once led. No longer admired. No longer celebrated. No longer welcomed. Instead, he had to walk covered and hidden, forced to distance himself from those who once followed him.

Why?

Because if he wasn't separated, he would infect those around him. His disease would spread.

This is an epidemic I've seen in the body of Christ—dysfunction breeds dysfunction. We love to shout and celebrate the words of Psalm 133:1, "Behold, how good and pleasant it is for brethren to dwell together in unity!" We love to talk about how the anointing flows down from the head to the rest of the body, like precious oil (Ps. 133:2).

But what if sickness flows down too?

What if dysfunction drips down just like the anointing?

According to Isaiah 1:5–6, "The whole head is sick, and the whole heart faints. From the sole of the foot even to the head, there is no soundness in it." If the head is sick, the whole body suffers. If a leader is infected, then those under his leadership become susceptible to the same dysfunction.

This was Naaman's reality.

With the appearance of one little red spot, this great commander—once powerful, admired, and respected—became a social outcast. Suddenly, all his achievements meant nothing.

This influential man of prominence, wealth, and military rank was suddenly plunged to such a low place in society that not even a slave would have traded places with him. All Naaman's accomplishments—his wealth, social position, and military rank—could neither insulate nor isolate him from this one devastating problem.

Now he was a leper.

Seen or unseen, I believe every person has some kind of dysfunction, character flaw, or weakness that they must face at some point in life. How they deal with it determines their future and their destiny.

Marked for Greatness

Have you ever seen someone who was marked for greatness yet burdened by dysfunction? A character flaw that slowly sabotaged their life, their ministry, their marriage, and their relationships?

Why does this happen?

Because the enemy will launch every attack possible against those who have been marked for greatness (John 10:10).

I believe dysfunction is the enemy's easiest and most effective weapon. Church history records many tragedies where the enemy has used dysfunction to derail those who had unique gifts and the call for greatness. His tactics have not changed (1 Pet. 5:8). Today, more than ever, I believe the devil still tries to use people's dysfunctions to defeat and derail them from their divine destiny.

> TODAY, MORE THAN EVER, I BELIEVE THE DEVIL STILL TRIES TO USE PEOPLE'S DYSFUNCTIONS TO DEFEAT AND DERAIL THEM FROM THEIR DIVINE DESTINY.

As you study this book, understand this:

- You are called by God (Rom. 8:30).
- You are marked for greatness (Jer. 1:5).

45

- God has equipped you with gifts, talents and a walk that is uniquely yours—to be used for His glory (1 Cor. 12:4–6).

But the enemy will exploit any dysfunction in you that remains undealt with to keep you from fulfilling all God has planned for your life.

God will not force you to face your dysfunction. It is your choice. Do you choose dysfunction—or destiny?

Prayer

Lord, I believe I am marked for greatness. Even though at times it may not look or feel like it, I believe I am! I know the enemy's attack on my life is an indication that I am marked for greatness. I refuse to allow a "but" to be added on to my identity, character, and accomplishments. In Jesus' name, amen.

Chapter 5

DYSFUNCTION OR DESTINY

I DO NOT BELIEVE the success of a ministry is measured by the size of the crowd. Nor is it marked by the number of names on a mailing list or followers on social media. Having been in church my entire life and serving as a lead pastor since the age of twenty-one, I have come to realize these things are insignificant from an eternal perspective. True ministry isn't about numbers; it is measured by the integrity, character, and spiritual health that the ministry imparts to its people.

I've seen it hundreds of times. People come to church, experience a touch from God, and for a moment, their heart begins to open. Excitement stirs. Faith rises. They rejoice and shout, convinced they've had a breakthrough—only to find themselves weeks later back in their same old mess, struggling with the same sin and dysfunction they've tried to deal with over and over.

In light of such stark contrasts, one might ask, "Did God really touch them?" The answer is "Yes." They sincerely sought prayer for their need, and God most certainly touched them. Yet, without real transformation, they return to the same old patterns, the same habits, the same ways of thinking. Much of what they experienced is an external touch with no real internal change.

True greatness is possible only when we allow God to heal our wounds and dysfunction.

As a pastor, it makes no difference to me how successful a person may be, or what their political, economic, or social status is. I don't care if they wear ripped blue jeans and a T-shirt or an expensive suit to church. What I care about most is the condition of their heart and character. I do not want to see anyone in my congregation stay sick, dysfunctional, bitter, or offended!

When we surrender our hurt and pain to Jesus with honesty and integrity, He will deal with the "dys" in our "function"—healing us from the inside out.

THE MEASURE OF SUCCESS

For Naaman, dysfunction took the form of leprosy. But let's take a deeper look into this disease—not from a natural point of view, but a symbolic one, referring to a dysfunction or a flaw in one's character.

> TRUE GREATNESS IS POSSIBLE ONLY WHEN WE ALLOW GOD TO HEAL OUR WOUNDS AND DYSFUNCTION.

When I talk about leprosy symbolically, I'm not speaking of a physical condition but rather of an emotional or spiritual condition. In my experience, great people are often prone to great dysfunction. It seems that the more God promotes someone, the more prevalent the dysfunction becomes. As the dysfunction develops into a stronghold, the enemy tightens his grip, using that one area to keep them from walking fully in their calling.

This is why choosing healing is critical—no matter the cost. Even when it's hard. Even when it hurts. In the end, it will be worth it.

Here's the thing: An individual cannot successfully continue to lead out of dysfunction. As Jesus so clearly pointed out in Luke 6:39, the blind cannot lead the blind lest they all fall into a ditch together.

Dysfunction will always sabotage destiny—unless you choose healing.

THE BOTTOM LINE

Now, think about this: Naaman was a leader, a commander, and a man of valor. Yet he was a leper (2 Kings 5:1).

Like Naaman, so it may be with you. At the end of the day, all the successes in the world will not matter if you have dysfunction.

Over the years, I have known highly successful individuals in ministry, yet insecurity consumed them. This led them to all kinds of destructive paths—some fell into adultery and immoral relationships, others misappropriated finances, and many found themselves in abusive relationships with their spouses. For some, their dysfunction poisoned their marriages, turning them into abusive fathers, or wives consumed by bitterness. Why? Because they were trying to fill a void—a void they thought could be filled with excellence, money, and success.

But that void can be filled only with Jesus.

So in Naaman's case, at the end of the day, who really

cared how great a man he was? Who cared how many people he led in his battalion? Who cared about his past victories and unmatched military expertise?

Scripture tells us the real point of the story, the bottom line...

"He was a leper."

The Eulogy of a Great Man

I would love it if someone would say of me today, "Pastor Jonathan Miller is a great man. He might not be the greatest pastor or preacher, he might not be the best dressed person, but he's a man of character." It is my earnest prayer that people would be able to say this of me every day that I live.

At the end of my life, it is my deepest desire that people would say, "Above all things, he was an honorable man. His entire life was marked with integrity and purity. He was a great leader, and people could trust his leadership."

The eulogy of a great man does not begin with all his admirable feats and valiant victories, only to end with "but he fell into sin and hurt a lot of people."

A truly great man does not have a *but* in his eulogy.

How would you like your eulogy to read?

Leading with Excellence

Mediocrity has no place in the life of a leader. There's a real sense of satisfaction in doing your best, and if you have been called to lead, excellence is essential.

Regarding Naaman, Scripture tells us that he was not just an average commander or leader—he was devoted to excellence. As I mentioned earlier, he was a great man of valor, which means he was brave and had the reputation of a hero. His bravery led to victory everywhere he went. Those whom he served considered him a great man, and those who served under him recognized him as a great leader too.

As a minister of the gospel, I believe my greatest responsibility is to impart the nature of Jesus Christ to all those I've been called to lead. His nature is not insecure, egotistical, or bitter. His nature is healthy, whole, and complete.

Every person Jesus healed, He left with this command: "Go and be made whole."

He didn't say, "Go and be a good Christian." He didn't say, "Go do good works and stay out of trouble." No—He said, "Go and be made whole."

THE ROAD TO WHOLENESS

We can learn much from the story of Naaman regarding the road to healing and wholeness. His accomplishments earned him notable recognition, yet it raises an interesting question: How would Naaman have been remembered if he had not been stricken with leprosy?

Would anyone ever have heard of him?

Charles H. Spurgeon, the great preacher, delivered over a hundred powerful sermons on the life of Job. He expressed similar thoughts about Job's legacy in one of his messages:

> Who would ever have heard of Job if he had not been tried? None would have said of him, "In all this Job sinned not." Only by his patience could

he be perfected and immortalized. Suppose that your record should be: from birth a sufferer, throughout life a struggler; at home a wrestler, and abroad a soldier and a cross-bearer; and, notwithstanding all this, full of joy and peace, through strong believing: tried to the uttermost, yet found faithful. In such a chronicle there is something worth remembering. There is no glory in being a feather-bed soldier, a man bedecked with gorgeous regimentals, but never beautified by a scar, or ennobled by a wound.[1]

BEGINNING THE JOURNEY

I believe Naaman's journey truly began with these five words: "...but he was a leper."

Up to this point, his "journey on life's road" had been paved with success, promotion, wealth, influence, recognition, and honor. He and his wife enjoyed a life of privilege, marked by social status, servants, and all the luxuries that accompanied it. Professionally, men looked to him for wisdom, instruction, protection, direction, and leadership.

Yet when a tiny red spot appeared on his skin, none of that could help him escape the cold, cruel fate that leprosy held for him. At that moment, he had two choices: dysfunction or destiny.

"Then Naaman went with his horses and chariot, and he stood at the door of Elisha's house" (2 Kings 5:9).

RESCUED BY A SLAVE

How ironic that God would use a young Hebrew slave girl, a servant in Naaman's household, to deliver a message of hope.

> And the Syrians had gone out on raids, and had brought back captive a young girl from the land of Israel. She waited on Naaman's wife. Then she said to her mistress, "If only my master were with the prophet who is in Samaria! For he would heal him of his leprosy."
> —2 Kings 5:2–3

When the young girl heard about Naaman's condition, she spoke of the prophet Elisha, telling him of the miracles that had happened through him. She confidently declared this prophet not only could—but would—cure her master of his leprosy!

Given his illness and status, it would have been far more convenient for Naaman to summon the prophet to come to him. Yet instead of demanding an audience, he humbled himself and traveled to where Elisha was.

When Naaman arrived at Elisha's residence, accompanied by his servants, his chariots, and his entourage, he likely anticipated a warm reception after his long journey. Surely, the prophet would greet him personally, honor his status, and perform a dramatic healing.

Yet when Naaman's servant knocked at the door, Elisha didn't bother to come out. Instead, he sent a messenger to the door with simple instructions: "Go and wash in the Jordan seven times, and your flesh shall be restored to you, and you shall be clean" (2 Kings 5:10).

Appalled and furious, Naaman stormed away.

"I can't believe it! I thought the prophet would come out of his house, call on the name of the Lord his God, wave his hand, and cure me of my leprosy! Instead, he sent a messenger to tell me to go wash in the Jordan River, a dirty river here in Israel. Surely the rivers in Damascus are better than any waters in Israel? Why couldn't I wash in them and be cleansed of this horrible disease?" (paraphrased from 2 Kings 5:11–12).

But his servants urged him to reconsider:

"Sir, if the prophet had told you to do something great, you would have done it, wouldn't you? Why not do as he instructed when he said, 'Wash and be clean'?" (paraphrased from 2 Kings 5:13).

So Naaman humbled himself.

> So he went down and dipped seven times in the Jordan, according to the saying of the man of God; and his flesh was restored like the flesh of a little child, and he was clean.
> —2 Kings 5:14

What an incredible moment! The same man who once led warriors into battle now stood humbly in the Jordan River, following the seemingly foolish instruction of a prophet he had never met face-to-face. But because of his obedience, he was made whole.

A Double Cure

Elisha wasn't intimidated by Naaman's reputation, his accomplishments, or his entourage. In fact, he didn't even take time to welcome him. Instead, he simply sent a

Dysfunction or Destiny

messenger with a conditional message: "If you want to be cleansed of your leprosy and have your flesh restored, go dip in the Jordan River seven times" (paraphrased from 2 Kings 5:10). Then, without further explanation, the messenger went back into the house and closed the door!

Naaman, angry and humiliated, was ready to leave. But as his servants reasoned with him, he finally humbled himself and agreed to do as the prophet directed. I wonder what was running through his mind as he climbed back into his chariot and headed toward the Jordan River. What did he feel as he stepped down and prepared to wade in the cold, murky waters?

Abandoning any preconceived notions, he took a step of obedience. The waters rose around him as he moved deeper in. With one final glance at those waiting for him back on the shore, he bent down and dipped into the Jordan. As he emerged, he probably examined his hands—still marked with leprosy.

Down again. A second time. A third. A fourth. A fifth. Carefully counting, the disciplined military man stayed focused on the task at hand. The chilly waters covered him once more. Dip number six. A quick glance at his servants watching from the shore, and then he leaned forward to take one final plunge into the Jordan. "So he went down and dipped seven times in the Jordan, according to the saying of the man of God; and his flesh was restored like the flesh of a little child, and he was clean" (2 Kings 5:14).

Finally, he completed the seventh dip. Perhaps time stood still as he fought the current to stand upright. As the water released its hold, the sun shone brighter, revealing his healed, restored body! He lifted his hands, studying them in amazement. Every finger was perfect with a healthy fingernail intact. He glanced down at his feet, and there they were—all ten toes, whole again. His skin was smooth, fresh, and new—just as the prophet had said. Naaman's leprosy was gone!

I believe Naaman's healing went far beyond the surface of his newly formed skin and restored body. Yes, his physical healing was evident, but there was another healing that took place. Remember, he was a great leader—but a prideful one. Naaman didn't just overcome leprosy—he overcame pride. "God resists the proud, but gives grace to the humble" (Jas. 4:6).

For the first time, he was not only a healthy man—he would also become a healthy leader. Getting the help he needed became more important than his rank, reputation, or past achievements. It may have hurt to heal, but for Naaman, it was worth it!

Church Hurt

As pastors, my wife and I have spoken with more people than we can count who have said, "We have suffered from church hurt." Many were once active members in their churches, faithfully serving and deeply involved. However, painful experiences left them wounded, hesitant to connect with a church like that again.

With compassion, we listen to the stories—many of which reveal legitimate hurt. Some discovered dysfunction within their leadership. Others suffered a form of abuse from spiritual authority. Some were wounded by fellow believers within the church community. Whatever the cause, their pain remained untreated, allowing it to fester and spread like an unchecked disease, eventually becoming what I call *the leprosy of offense*.

Perhaps you too have experienced church hurt—wounds that have been left untreated, giving way to offense. But I have good news for you. Keep reading! You can experience freedom. You can be made whole.

Leadership and Leprosy

When a church leader has a *leprous dysfunction* in their life, it will inevitably affect those under their leadership. Maybe their dysfunction is insecurity. As it progresses, insecurity eats away at their flesh, causing them to take everything as a personal attack or to place unrealistic expectations on others.

Eventually, they say and do things that wound those who serve under them, infecting them with a *leprosy* that damages and eats away at their emotions. If these wounds remain unhealed, they will lead only to more dysfunction, affecting more people.

Has a church leader hurt you? If so, it is of vital importance that you seek healing from your wounds, or you may find yourself wounding others instead of being the person God has called you to be.

You Are Called

You have been called to greatness, not mediocrity. You were not created just to occupy a seat at church and satisfy some religious duty for the week. As a believer, you have been called to lead others to Christ, to bring them into freedom.

You may never stand on a stage, hold a microphone in

your hand, or deliver a sermon. However, the moment you surrendered your heart to Jesus, these words became your mandate:

> Go into all the world and preach the gospel to every creature.
> —Mark 16:15

Regardless of what life has thrown at you, you have a God-ordained destiny. You are called to share the precious gospel of Jesus Christ and bring the lost into the kingdom. You are called to produce fruit. You are called to set captives free. You are called to lay hands on the sick and see them recover. You have been called to greatness, not mediocrity.

> The Spirit of the Lord God is upon Me, because the Lord has anointed Me to preach good tidings to the poor; He has sent Me to heal the brokenhearted, to proclaim liberty to the captives, and the opening of the prison to those who are bound.
> —Isaiah 61:1

As a believer, you have been called to be a leader. Your role as a leader is reminiscent of a shepherd—one who carefully watches over the sheep, guides them to green pastures where they can be fed, leads them to cool brooks where they can be refreshed, and rescues lost lambs from danger (Ps. 23:1–3).

But just as a shepherd must be strong and capable to tend his flock, so must you be whole and healed to effectively lead. If a shepherd is weak or injured, relying on his staff as a crutch rather than a tool, the well-being of the sheep is at risk.

Likewise, leadership qualities are evident wherever you are—they are not dependent upon your surroundings. Your gifts and calling will shine whether you are leading in a ministry role or simply being a good example of integrity and faith to your coworkers. When you experience healing from past hurts and are liberated from yesterday's dysfunction, people will recognize the freedom in you and realize that they need to follow you to get to Jesus.

But as your healing draws people closer to Jesus, your unhealed areas can also lead them astray. If you are afflicted with dysfunctional leprosy, it will affect your ability to lead and inevitably affect those who are following you. "Can the blind lead the blind? Will they not both fall into the ditch?" (Luke 6:39)

If you are blinded by unhealed wounds, you will falter, and after you fall into the ditch, those following you will fall with you. When you crash, they crash. When your life falls apart, their lives fall apart.

> WHEN YOU EXPERIENCE HEALING FROM PAST HURTS AND ARE LIBERATED FROM YESTERDAY'S DYSFUNCTION, PEOPLE WILL RECOGNIZE THE FREEDOM IN YOU AND REALIZE THAT THEY NEED TO FOLLOW YOU TO GET TO JESUS.

Our constant prayer must be "God, heal us and set us free. Heal us that we might lead with effectiveness."

The Fear Factor

So many people are afraid. They operate in fear, making decisions hastily out of fear. Too often, some of these people are in church leadership. Instead of imparting security, they promote insecurity. Instead of instilling stability, they create instability.

I do my best to make decisions slowly. Sure, some circumstances require immediate action, but it's always better when you have a measured reaction. However, I have seen pastors who are quick to react without much thought, often out of fear, emotion, or impulse rather than wisdom. This creates a sense of uncertainty and instability, leaving people in the church asking themselves questions like...

- When will my last day be?
- When will I be removed from my position?
- When will I be mishandled?

Many in the church come in Sunday morning looking so righteous and holy, yet deep down, they're scared to death—waiting for the very thing they fear to happen. Wouldn't it be refreshing to come into a church and feel secure enough to be honest? Wouldn't it be nice if church were a place where you didn't have to pretend, where you could admit, "I'm struggling. I need help"?

Part of our code at our church is "Keepin' It Real—We Are All Messed Up." The reason this resonates so deeply with our church family is that, too often, the church has not provided a safe place for people to be real. But the truth is, no matter how much we love Jesus, you and I are imperfect people who daily need God's mercy and grace. We might as well be honest about it!

I know that no matter my calling, title, or position, I too need help! I must constantly examine areas of dysfunction in my own life. Sometimes healing seems like a never-ending process.

Even though I deal with dysfunction, I refuse to let dysfunction be in the driver's seat of my decisions. Like anyone else, I will never achieve a state of perfection, but I can walk in enough freedom to keep dysfunction from being in control of my life.

It takes functional people to reach dysfunctional people. Healed, whole, and functional people are needed to reach the hurting, the broken, and the dysfunctional. You are either one or the other!

Mountains Too Big to Climb

When I was twelve years old, my family faced a challenge that seemed impossible to overcome. Our lives completely fell apart, and through the circumstances we endured, we quickly realized just how much "dys" was in front of our "function." We were heartsick, desperate, and unsure of what to do. So we turned to pastors, leaders, and others in the ministry for guidance—only to find that most of them were worse off than we were!

Without going into unnecessary detail, the situation put my father in a precarious position, leaving my family and me to deal with the *mountain of opportunity* before us. Each time we sought help, we came in, symbolically rolled up our sleeves, and said, "Look! Check out our leprosy! Can you tell us what to do to be whole?"

But time and time again, we found that many of those we looked to for answers were struggling with their own leprosy, their own dysfunctions. And it didn't take long to recognize it. Instead of finding the help we needed, we encountered leaders who were just as broken, just as wounded.

Thankfully, the Holy Spirit became our guide in a continuous journey to health and freedom. I thank God for giving my family the tools to discover the kind of healing I am writing about in this book. What He did for us, He can do for you.

My Desire for You

I want to see you be everything God has called you to be. I don't want you at the end of your life to look back with regret, knowing you got only *half* of it right. I want to see you walk in the fullness of your destiny—nothing missing, nothing lacking—rather than falling short because of sabotaging dysfunction.

It's my heart to see you healed so that you can impart that healing to others. When you're free, you help set others free. When you're whole, you make room for others to be whole too. That's what this is all about!

Prayer

> *Heavenly Father, I am ready to walk the road of wholeness. I don't want a "but" attached to my eulogy. Fear will have no hold on me. With integrity, I will acknowledge my weaknesses and areas of dysfunction. I will trust the Holy Spirit to lead and guide in this journey to freedom. In Jesus' name, amen.*

Chapter 6

MESSY LIFE, MESSY PEOPLE

As I said before, one of our church codes is "Keepin' It Real—We Are All Messed Up." Life is messy, and it's filled with messy people—including you and me. Another part of our code reassures us that God causes "Messes to Become Miracles." So, if your life is messy right now and you feel all messed up, be encouraged because your messes are about to become miracles!

No one is exempt from messes. We each must deal with our human frailties while on earth. But too often we expect certain people to be *mess-free*—especially those in spiritual leadership. We experience the anointing upon their lives. We witness the powerful gifts of God flowing through them. Then we are shocked when we discover their personal lives are in absolute chaos. *How did this happen? How can someone this anointed be so messed up? Why did they do what they did? How did they get into such sin?*

Have you been disappointed by someone you've known and respected for years? Maybe you found out they abuse their wife or their children. Maybe they cheated on their spouse, and now they're getting a divorce. Maybe you learned of some other moral failure, and you just can't believe it. *How can such good people do such bad things?* Disillusioned, you wrestle with the reality that people you looked up to have fallen.

The truth is, life is messy. People are messy. And, unfortunately, when messed-up people are in their greatest hour of need, the church often has no idea how to help them—so they turn away.

In Mark 5, there's an account of a man with an unclean spirit who lived among the tombs. Demon-possessed, he lacked even the ability to *want* to be free. Scripture tells us he had often been bound with fetters and chains and had shaken them off, and no man could tame or control him.

But "when he saw Jesus from afar, he ran and worshiped Him" (Mark 5:6). The anointing was greater than his own will and desire, and his freedom began as he saw Jesus from afar.

Why don't we ask the Holy Spirit to draw us in the same way—to pull us toward freedom even in the areas of our lives in which we don't necessarily want it?

We explored Michal and David's love story in earlier chapters. Michal, deeply in love, told her father, King Saul, about her feelings. Saul saw this as an opportunity—not to bless her marriage but to use her love as bait to kill David. When Saul's men came for David, Michal helped him escape, deceiving them by pretending he was sick in bed. Her love for David led her to lie and risk everything, even standing against her own father.

Have you ever lied or covered up for someone close to you? Maybe it looked something like this:

Question: "Why wasn't your husband at church this morning?"

Audible response: "Something unexpected came up."

Honest answer: "He slept in and is going fishing."

Here's another example:

Question: "Your wife seems really quiet today. Is everything OK with her?"

Audible response: "Yes, she just has a lot on her mind right now."

Honest answer: "We're in the middle of one of the biggest fights of our marriage!"

Even when it's not consequential, we instinctively know how to cover for those we love.

Michal's love for David led her to choose him over her father, but Saul punished her by giving her to another man. David, however, pursued her. He risked everything—even his position—to bring her back.

Yet, in 2 Samuel 6, when Michal sees David dancing before the Lord as he brings the ark of the covenant back, she despises him in her heart. "Now as the ark of the LORD came into the City of David, Michal, Saul's daughter, looked through a window and saw King David leaping and whirling before the LORD; and she despised him in her heart" (2 Sam. 6:16).

How did the woman who once risked everything for David end up here? I believe this shift in her heart stems from unresolved generational issues. David never addressed the dysfunction she inherited from her father. Michal never confronted it either.

What once *drew* her to David—his passion for God—now *repelled* her. Why? Because undealt-with iniquity will always produce a mess. And in our lives, if we don't allow God to deal with our generational dysfunctions, our messes will continue to multiply.

Dealing with the Mess

I've seen this happen in marriages—two people fall madly in love, get married, and then, several years later, they turn into bitter rivals. The passion that once bound them together now fuels their resentment and mistrust. How does this happen? More often than not, like Michal and David, they failed to identify and confront generational iniquities that ultimately sabotaged their relationship.

> AND IN OUR LIVES, IF WE DON'T ALLOW GOD TO DEAL WITH OUR GENERATIONAL DYSFUNCTIONS, OUR MESSES WILL CONTINUE TO MULTIPLY.

If it hasn't already, iniquity will sabotage every relationship in your life unless you are willing to stand in integrity and say, "Lord, reveal any area of iniquity in me, and make me free."

The Man with the Withered Hand

In Luke 6, Jesus entered the synagogue to teach, and among those present was a man with a serious issue—his hand was withered. The religious leaders watched closely, waiting to see if Jesus would heal him on the Sabbath day, a day of rest and not works.

> Now it happened on another Sabbath, also, that He entered the synagogue and taught. And a man was there whose right hand was withered. So the scribes and Pharisees watched Him closely, whether He would heal on the Sabbath, that they might find an accusation against Him.
> —LUKE 6:6–7

The word *withered* suggests his hand may have been injured, possibly even burned by fire. In this fallen world, many of us have been burned—wounded by betrayal, rejection, or circumstances beyond our control. These "fires" don't just scar our past; they shape our present and threaten our future.

Remember how easy it was for you to love before you were hurt? How open and trusting you were before you experienced betrayal? Maybe, since being burned, you've become guarded, hesitant, unwilling to trust again. Perhaps life's fires have changed you—once happy and carefree, now cautious and withdrawn. Have you lost your ability to play, to have fun, to serve at church, to connect with others? Have the wounds of your past withered a part of who you are?

I've seen people who long to open up, who want to love and be vulnerable, yet they won't allow themselves. They are overwhelmed by isolation, trapped behind walls built of fear. A painful fire in their past has caused a "withering," leaving them hiding in the shadows.

Filled with compassion, Jesus looked at the man with the withered hand and commanded, "Stand up." Perhaps the man felt a wave of shame, hesitant to expose the very thing that made him feel weak and different. I don't know how he felt, but I can only imagine how I would have felt. If it were me, I probably would have stood with my hand tucked inside my garments, doing my best to keep my shame hidden.

After the man stood up, Jesus boldly said, "Stretch out your hand" (Luke 6:10). Not just any hand—his withered hand. "Show me the place that's been burned with fire. Uncover your wound. Expose what you are most ashamed of." Why? Because healing begins with honesty. Transformation happens when we stop hiding. Transparency always precedes transformation.

Many today would have responded differently. They would have stretched out the good hand, keeping the withered one hidden, denying they even had a problem. But this man obeyed. He stretched forth the very thing he wanted to conceal, and the moment he did—he was healed. His withered hand was restored in an instant. "And he did so, and his hand was restored as whole as the other" (Luke 6:10).

> BECAUSE HEALING BEGINS WITH HONESTY, TRANSFORMATION HAPPENS WHEN WE STOP HIDING. TRANSPARENCY ALWAYS PRECEDES TRANSFORMATION.

By stretching forth his hand, he was saying, "This is me. This is my ugly, burned, deformed hand. See my dysfunction. See my brokenness." We must possess the same integrity about our internal condition as this man possessed with his external one. "Here I am, Lord. I've been hurt, and now I'm bitter, insecure, angry, and afraid. I used to love people. But now I hate everyone. This is who I've become, and it's not very pretty."

This man had the courage to expose his greatest weakness to Jesus, and in doing so, he found healing. No more hiding. No more shame. No more barriers. It hurt to heal, but it was worth it.

Wholeness is available to everyone—but if you don't think this message is for you, you're getting this journey started off on the wrong foot. Keep it real—we are all messed up. Even you. Everyone struggles with some area of dysfunction—messed-up thinking, insecurity, fear, unforgiveness, bitterness, rejection, abandonment. Whatever it is, you don't have to stay withered. Healing is waiting. The only question is—will you stretch it forth?

LIBERATED AND FREE INDEED

If you refuse to be real with yourself and with God, your leprosy—your dysfunction—will remain untreated. Eventually, it will begin to affect those around you. Maybe it hasn't happened yet, or maybe it already has. Either way, it's time to break the cycle. It's time to heal! As much as your dysfunction negatively impacts others, your healing will have a positive effect. Your healing isn't just for *you*—it's for *everyone* connected to you. When you find freedom, it spills over into the lives of your spouse, your children, your friends, and your church.

"Therefore if the Son makes you free, you shall be free indeed" (John 8:36).

What does that mean? It means *total* freedom. Not partial. Not halfway. *All the way.* Every part of your life—your mind, your emotions, your relationships—fully healed and set free.

We read earlier in 2 Kings 5:9, "Then Naaman went with his horses and chariot, and he stood at the door of Elisha's house." Now, let me ask you—are *you* standing at the door? That door was the place of Naaman's divine appointment. That door positioned him for healing.

Are you willing to leave behind what's comfortable? Are you ready to step out of the familiar and into the unknown? Are you willing to get out of your chariot—out of your place of control, out of your guarded and protected environment? Staying where you've been feels safe. But healing *requires* you to do the uncomfortable.

Are you ready to walk down from your chariot and step up to the door you've never knocked on before?

It's Go Time!

Maybe you've been wounded by someone close—a mother, a father, a close friend, a spouse, or another family member. Or perhaps you've been burned by a church leader, and now you've completely turned your back on church. Maybe you've even distanced yourself from *God* altogether.

You might still attend church from time to time, but when you do, you sit there feeling disconnected—detached from the people around you, detached from worship, and most of all, detached from *Him*. Something happened that hurt you, and now, without even realizing it, you've drifted away from God.

Or perhaps you suffered an abusive relationship that left you wounded, distorting your ability to trust, making you hypersensitive, easily offended, always on guard—living in defense mode because you're convinced that people either want to hurt you or have ulterior motives.

Has the leprosy in your life caused your passion for the things of God to grow cold? Has your relationship with Him grown distant? Is He no longer number one in your life?

If Jesus Christ is not Lord of all, *He's not Lord at all.* "But why do you call me 'Lord, Lord,' and not do the things which I say?" (Luke 6:46).

I am asking you today—do you have the boldness of the man in the synagogue to stretch forth your withered hand to the Master? Will you say, "It's me, Lord. Here's my mess. Here's my dysfunction. I want to come back to You. Heal me and make me whole"?

The First Step

Are you ready to take the first step? Are you ready to rekindle that passionate relationship with Jesus Christ? Are you ready to allow God to awaken every dormant area in your heart? Are you ready to live and enjoy the abundant life He promised? "I have come that they may have life, and that they may have it more abundantly" (John 10:10).

Everything can change today. You don't have to let dysfunction create distance between you and God. Without hesitation, push through the pain, the shame, the guilt, and the embarrassment. Stop covering up your brokenness—and stretch forth every withered area to Jesus. *He will make you whole!*

Maybe you're reading this book and you've never had

a personal relationship with Jesus. If that's you, I have great news—Jesus loves you and desires for you to be whole. But how do you enter this relationship with Him?

John 14:6 says, "Jesus said to him, 'I am the way, the truth, and the life. No one comes to the Father except through Me.'" Romans 10:13 says, "Whoever calls on the name of the Lord shall be saved."

Let's pray this prayer together.

Prayer

Dear Jesus, I give You my life. I give You every part of me. I repent of my sins and ask that You forgive me and make me a new person. I believe that You died on a cross for my sins and that You were raised from the dead with all might, power, and authority. I confess with my mouth and believe in my heart that You are my Lord and Savior. From this day on, I will live for You. Amen.

Chapter 7

IRRITATION: A PART OF THE PROCESS

Early in my ministry, I traveled as an evangelist, accepting invitations to various churches each month. During that time, a man by the name of Mark Arthur traveled with me. Mark has been in my life since I was five years old, and to this day he remains one of my family's closest friends.

One of Mark's duties was giving me a breath mint before the time of personal ministry at the end of services. There's nothing worse than an evangelist whose breath overwhelms you with the remnants of last night's meal!

Even though Mark was diligent, he had one problem. He kept giving me extra-large mints. I often joked with him, saying, "Do you know how difficult it is to pray for someone when you have this oversized mint in your mouth?"

Despite all my complaints, Mark continued to provide me with these extra-large mints every time we were on the road. If you ever get the chance to know Mark, you would probably agree with me that he most likely kept doing it on purpose. One night, I was passionately praying over a man, and before I knew it, the oversized mint went flying out of my mouth at what seemed to be 3,000 miles per hour. *Bam!*

The mint hit him right in the face. One minute I was praying with passion, and suddenly everything shifted.

Perhaps in your life you have experienced sudden shifts. You watch the change unfold in what seems like slow motion, but it is happening so fast that you cannot do anything about it. Like me and my unexpectedly airborne mint, you are stunned and cannot believe what just happened.

On another occasion, I was invited to speak at a men's conference in Cincinnati, Ohio. I was obviously excited about the conference, but as a bonus, the conference just so happened to be next door to one of my favorite amusement parks!

The conference went great, and afterward, we even had time to head over to the amusement park. As my friends and I were exiting the conference, a man ran up to me and said, "Jonathan, can I pray for you? There's something God wants me to do."

Being a pastor's kid, I've been around long enough to recognize, by the strange look in his eyes and the tone of his voice, that this could take a while, and it could get weird! As he began his prayer, he commanded, "Close your eyes and lift your hands." (In those days, I was much more inclined to allow people to overstep boundaries.)

I reluctantly closed my eyes and lifted my hands. Apparently, my "cooperation" fueled the situation as I heard him say, "This may sound strange, but I have to be obedient to what God is saying." He began to "anoint" my eyes, my ears, and my mouth.

But I quickly realized that the substance on his fingers was not oil—it was saliva from his mouth! Yes, this man put his fingers in his mouth, then put them all over my face! The "friends" who were with me did absolutely nothing to stop this. When I opened my eyes to see where they were, all their eyes were closed as if they were in deep prayer. That moment is definitely one I'll never forget!

A Little Mud and a Miracle

The incidents above gave me a new perspective on the account of the blind man and the pool of Siloam:

> When He [Jesus] had said these things, He spat on the ground and made clay with the saliva; and He anointed the eyes of the blind man with the clay. And He said to him, "Go, wash in the pool of Siloam" (which is translated, Sent). So he went and washed, and came back seeing.
> —John 9:6–7, Emphasis Added

To my knowledge, no miracle occurred from my flying mint or that spit-covered intrusion, but these experiences helped me gain insight into how the blind man must have felt. His world was cloaked in darkness, he was totally vulnerable to those around him, and he had no way to anticipate what was about to happen to him.

Scripture doesn't tell us how long Jesus took to blend the spittle with the clay, but when it was just right, He carefully took the mixture and anointed the blind man's eyes. The blind man was probably stunned as Jesus spread the unidentifiable moist mixture of clay and spit on his eyes. He then instructed him to go wash in the pool of Siloam. "So he went and washed, and came back seeing" (John 9:7).

The Bible doesn't say whether someone helped the blind man make his way to the pool of Siloam, nor does it indicate how he was able to negotiate his way down the rough, rocky steps to the water. But when he arrived and washed his eyes, his darkness was dispelled. The Bible says he "came back seeing" (John 9:7).

Let's look more closely at the account of this blind man's healing. First, Jesus used an unconventional method to bring sight to his eyes—He spat on the ground and made clay with His saliva. There were probably tiny grains of sand mixed into the clay. In the natural, it seems that this combination would be irritating and potentially injurious to the eyes—not a likely cure for blindness.

As the blind man waited in the darkness of his familiar world, he likely tried to distinguish what was happening around him by the sounds he heard. When the mixture was ready to use, Jesus scooped it up and smeared the rough, irritating mud over his eyes, probably pressing it firmly in place. Then He told the blind man to go wash in the pool of Siloam.

As the blind man washed the gritty, muddy mixture from his eyes, his lifelong dysfunction vanished. His eyes received their sight, and for the first time, he beheld the world around him as it truly was.

"Therefore the neighbors and those who previously had seen that he was blind, said, 'Is not this he who sat and begged?'" (John 9:8).

Secondly, when the once-blind man returned home,

Irritation: A Part of the Process

those who knew him were surprised by what they saw and questioned, "Is this the blind man who sat begging?" There was no logical explanation for how this man who was born blind could now see. They marveled at the miracle!

Inevitably, this miraculous event not only brought the blind man his physical sight but also freed him from a life of dependence on his family, his neighborhood, and society.

In biblical times, those who were blind often wore a distinguishing garment. This allowed the public to recognize them, as it was customary to provide food, shelter, and assistance. However, having received his sight, this formerly blind man was finally able to care for himself and provide for his own needs, fully healed and whole.

DEALING WITH YOUR DYSFUNCTION

It is important to note that the Lord deals with each of us on an individual basis, even if the dysfunction appears to be the same. In Mark 10:46, we find the account of another blind man—Bartimaeus—who sat by the roadside outside Jericho, begging for money and food. As the sound of an approaching crowd grew louder, Bartimaeus discovered that Jesus of Nazareth was approaching and began to cry out, "Jesus, Son of David, have mercy on me!" (Mark 10:47). When the crowd tried to silence him, he cried out even louder, hoping that Jesus would hear him.

As the crowd pressed forward, attempting to silence Bartimaeus, I imagine they tried to remind him of his labels. I can almost hear them saying, "Bartimaeus, you are blind! You are poor! Jesus doesn't have time for you!

You cannot and will not change." The world labels us the same way: *You have depression. You are an alcoholic. You are too messed up. You have ruined your life. You are and you will be...*(Add your own scenario here.)

Don't let those voices in the crowd silence your cry! Don't let those voices convince you that you are disqualified! The very things the enemy says disqualify you are the very things that qualify you for God to move!

As the commotion of the crowd continued, Jesus heard the persistent cry of Bartimaeus. Scripture tells us, "So Jesus stood still and commanded him to be called. Then they called the blind man, saying to him, 'Be of good cheer. Rise, He is calling you'" (Mark 10:49).

But before blind Bartimaeus was led to Jesus, he did something significant—he threw away his garment. This act was an expression of his faith in Jesus' power to heal and restore his sight. That garment was the standard worn by blind individuals, distinguishing him as dependent on others for assistance in day-to-day activities and provision.

As Bartimaeus cast aside his garment and approached Jesus, he left behind his past and his dependence on the natural world. Then he heard Jesus say, "What do you want Me to do for you?" (Mark 10:51). Without hesitation, Bartimaeus responded with faith, "Rabboni, that I may receive my sight" (Mark 10:51). "Then Jesus said to him, 'Go your way; your faith has made you well.' And immediately he received his sight and followed Jesus on the road." (Mark 10:52)

Jesus recognized his faith and commanded, "Go your way; your faith has made you whole." By faith, Bartimaeus received his sight instantly and was made whole.

GOD USES IRRITATION TO HEAL

In the account of the blind man at the pool of Siloam, Jesus employed a different approach, applying a muddy wet paste to his eyes (John 9:6). How could this bring comfort or healing? Yet, just like this blind man, isn't it amazing that God allows you and me to be put in the most uncomfortable situations and then says, "I want you to be healed"?

Healing hurts.

When people reach a place where they are willing to admit they are offended and need help, they often resist the method God chooses. Instead of the Lord causing their offenses to supernaturally vanish, He seemingly allows even greater offenses to arise— as if to give them another opportunity to deal with the offense the right way

> SOMETIMES OUR IRRITANT IS A REMINDER THAT WE NEED GOD.

since they missed the mark in the past. Sadly, when new irritation arises, people often lose the battle, failing to realize that God is providing them another chance to confront their giants.

Sometimes our irritant is a reminder that we need God.

God has a way of placing us in the most uncomfortable, unfamiliar, and irritating situations to reveal our dysfunction and give us an opportunity to find healing.

Have you ever noticed that, at times, certain things just seem to rub you the wrong way? Someone can look at you a certain way, and you just want to go off!

This can happen with your spouse, your kids, or your coworkers. They might say something as simple as "Good morning," and rather than responding kindly, you mutter an abrupt response and hastily leave the room. You find yourself irritated for no apparent reason.

Sometimes it takes very little to make you angry because you're already on edge. You're so volatile that the smallest thing can cause you to erupt in anger. Just a tiny bump or a little nudge sends you into an explosion. Yet I've observed time and time again how God chooses moments of great irritation to release great healing.

Remember, *it's not in comfort that we're healed, it's in discomfort.* It is in the midst of great pain and unease that the Holy Spirit reveals things we would never notice in an easy, comfortable place. "My brothers, count it all joy when you fall into diverse temptations, knowing that the trying of your faith develops patience" (Jas. 1:2–3, MEV).

Have you ever discovered something about yourself that you didn't realize until you faced an uncomfortable, difficult situation?

For example, you may have thought you had your temper under control—until someone disrespected you, talked badly about you, or walked out on you. Then suddenly, something ugly rises up. You might even question, "Where did this come from? That's not me!"

> REMEMBER, IT'S NOT IN COMFORT THAT WE'RE HEALED, IT'S IN DISCOMFORT.

Oh, yes, it is! That problem was always there. It just took some irritation to get it to the surface. For example,

Irritation: A Part of the Process

if a glass is full, you'll find out what's in it with just the slightest bump. Likewise, we know what's in us by what comes out of us when life bumps us with difficulties and uncomfortable circumstances.

I have discovered God often allows irritants in our lives to act as sandpaper—smoothing out our rough edges. Have you ever noticed that there are some people around you whom you just can't seem to get away from? They have a way of grating on your nerves, almost like sandpaper.

Sometimes this sandpaper comes in the form of a spiritual leader, a spouse, a coworker, or even a friend. You may find yourself doing everything you can to distance yourself from them, but it seems there's no escape!

Have you considered that God has placed these irritants in your life for a reason?

Just like sandpaper smooths out rough wood, those who irritate us are sent to refine our personalities. These people aren't obstacles to healing—they are a necessity of the healing process.

THE POWER OF IRRITATION

There have been times in my life when spiritual leaders have irritated me by saying things like, "You have a problem area that needs to be addressed." Ugh, who likes to hear those words?

On one specific occasion, I remember hearing these words: "I want to talk to you about pride." Taken aback, I responded, "If there's an area of pride in my life, I don't see it. Please show me."

I'll never forget the response I received. "I don't see a

lot of pride in you now," they said, "but I want to address it before it becomes an even bigger issue." Sometimes spiritual authority will proactively address issues before they have a chance to develop in your life.

Even though I felt the love and concern of this individual, I have to admit, I also felt a little irritated. Have you ever felt that sinking feeling in the pit of your stomach when you know you're about to face an uncomfortable truth? That's exactly how I felt.

Before I knew it, I was on the defensive, making it very clear how much I did not have a pride problem. Suddenly, I recognized how strongly I was reacting and realized that I obviously had more of a problem with pride than I thought. Had it not been for that irritating conversation, I might never have seen it.

I'm so grateful that God used irritation to expose this area of pride in me. As soon as it was identified, I repented, and the process of overcoming it began.

Pulling a One-Eighty

Sometimes the Lord will use a sudden and unexpected 180-degree turn in a relationship to expose areas of dysfunction and unresolved issues, even though, at the time, we may not recognize it as God-ordained.

Have you ever seen a situation where someone does everything they can to get involved in leadership, start a ministry in the church, or seek a position on staff? They are there every time the doors are open. They're consistent. They're punctual. They're great at what they do. They have favor with the pastor and other church leaders. Before long, they have become such a vital asset to the ministry.

Irritation: A Part of the Process

But then something changes. Other volunteers and new model members begin to step up, shifting the dynamic in relationships. Now they're no longer the only ones arriving early. Others are just as punctual and equally gifted in what they bring to the table. This 180-degree shift causes them to feel hurt, left out, and unimportant. They begin struggling to recapture what seems to be their lost role because they are no longer "the one."

As a pastor, I've noticed that—whether due to circumstances or the busyness of life—there are times when I'm simply unable to maintain the same closeness in certain relationships. It's not intentional; it's just how things unfold. In most cases, the people I have relationships with have understood the natural ebbs and flows of life, but others, who struggle with insecurity, often take it as a personal affront. This becomes evident when people say things like, "You don't love me anymore! How could you do this to me? You've changed!" Instead of recognizing it's just a shift in season, their insecurities distort the narrative, making it about them.

The distance ultimately exposes an overdependence and deep-rooted insecurity.

I have also seen spiritual leaders create distance from certain people—often without any reason or plausible explanation. Perhaps you've been on the receiving end of this. If so, I truly hurt for you. However, the real question is, what did your response to this situation reveal about you? Was your reaction appropriate, or was it out of balance? Were you hurt, or did it feel like your entire world collapsed? Were you disappointed, or were you completely devastated? Perhaps these responses indicate that you are overly needy and struggling with deep insecurities.

God has a way of bringing our hidden struggles to the surface. Even in areas where we feel confident and believe we've "arrived," God gently reminds us that we still have more healing to experience. When you find yourself in frustrating situations or surrounded by people who irritate you, remember: God may be leading you into a greater level of healing. Be quick to recognize. Be quick to repent.

Sand in Your Eyes

Have you ever gotten sand in your eyes? Maybe at the beach or on a windy day? Even though you didn't see the almost invisible particles of sand coming your way, you immediately realized they were there the moment they lodged in your eyes.

When something irritates your eye, what's your first reaction? If you are like me, before you even think about it, you instinctively try to rub it away. Of course, rubbing only makes it worse, intensifying the irritation and discomfort. Yet this is still the first reaction of most of us. We try to fix it. But the harder we try, the worse it becomes.

More than likely, the clay mixture Jesus put on the blind man's eyes had a similar effect. He must have felt an overwhelming urge to remove it immediately. Yet he did not. Maybe he understood that if he interfered, it would only cause more pain. He yielded to the Master's process, waiting for further instruction instead of trying to fix it himself.

Irritation: A Part of the Process

Don't try to dictate the terms and conditions of your process. God is the God of process. Trust Him to lead you and carry you through it. Keep your hands out of the mix. After all, when you tried to "help" yourself in the past, did it really work out for the best?

Allow me to explain further. I can't count how many times I have seen people ignore the instructions of wise counsel—guidance that lays out a clear path for healing. Instead, they take matters into their own hands. I've been guilty of this too. Human nature craves control. Even if it's "I'll follow 90 percent of the plan, but I'll handle 10 percent my way." Anything to maintain a sense of control.

You know what that does? It disrupts the entire process. It prolongs the need for healing. Keep your hands to yourself, no matter how much it itches and burns. Don't try to remove the irritation prematurely. Receive your instructions, start the process, and stay in it until you are whole.

It hurts to heal, but it's worth it!

PRAYER

Heavenly Father, help me to understand the power of irritation. Help me to be thankful for irritation. Even though it is uncomfortable, I know You are using it to help bring about my healing. I am willing to embrace discomfort so I can realize wholeness. Strengthen my faith to keep my hands out of the mix. I place my life in Your hands. In Jesus' name, amen.

Chapter 8

STAY WHERE YOU'RE SENT

WHEN I WAS a young child, I suffered from deep embarrassment. I was incredibly shy and struggled to even say hello to people. I was extremely quiet and reserved. If I was ever asked a question, I could never bring myself to stand in front of a crowd, let alone speak to one. If I had to do any of these things, my palms would instantly sweat, and my face would flush bright red.

I'll never forget the night it happened. It was a Sunday night, and my dad called me up for prayer in front of the entire church. Immediately, my palms began sweating, and my face turned beet red, but by the end of that prayer, every trace of embarrassment was completely gone! To this day, there's still no trace of it!

When sharing this struggle-turned-testimony, most people can't believe it was me. But that's what happens when God does a complete and total work of healing—there will be no trace of that dysfunction in your life.

When true, complete, and total transformation comes to your life, it can be difficult for some people to acknowledge and accept. Bottom line—sometimes transformation is so extreme that there's no trace of your past left behind.

When people try to improve through human effort, they say, "I'm getting better." But as long as you're getting better, there's still a trace of dysfunction. By contrast, when you allow the Lord to heal you through His sovereign power, you will become completely unrecognizable to those around you.

When God performs a sovereign and total work of healing, there will be no trace of that dysfunction left in your life!

Recognizing Your Sent Place

In John 9:7 Jesus met the blind man at the pool of Siloam, "and He said to him, 'Go, wash in the pool of Siloam' (which is translated, Sent). So he went and washed, and came back seeing."

But why Siloam? Siloam means *Sent Place*.[1]

When the blind man obeyed and went to his *Sent Place* to wash, not only was the irritation cleansed from his eyes, but he was also made whole from the dysfunction that had plagued him his entire life. However, he did not receive the miracle of his sight until he went to his *Sent Place*.

> WHEN GOD PERFORMS A SOVEREIGN AND TOTAL WORK OF HEALING, THERE WILL BE NO TRACE OF THAT DYSFUNCTION LEFT IN YOUR LIFE!

Your *Sent Place* isn't just any old place. It's not

somewhere you choose on a whim, and more often than not, it won't be a place of comfort. It is the place God has ordained for you. I believe this place is directly connected to your destiny, where you will find your healing: in spirit, soul, and body.

Recognizing your *Sent Place* is crucial because if you fail to do so, you may end up wasting precious time wandering into the wrong places. For example, if God has called you to a specific church, but you choose to attend another church based on personal preference, you may have unknowingly delayed your healing process.

I love the church I lead, and I believe that New Beginnings is one of the greatest churches in Orlando. Yet as wonderful as it is, it would be a waste of your time if it were not your *Sent Place*. Only in your *Sent Place* will you receive the specific kind of ministry you need to experience healing and breakthrough.

I want to give you three key indicators to help you identify your *Sent Place*:

1. A place of integrity: Do they care more about your character than they do about your gift? In other words, are they committed to discipling you, challenging you, and helping you grow at all costs—ensuring you become the best "you" you can be?

2. A place of safety: Are you able to be yourself? Can you be real? Is it safe to be vulnerable? Is it a place where, even when you're being challenged, being stretched, or

walking through difficult seasons, you feel secure and loved?

3. A place of growth: Are you being stretched? Are you being challenged? Are you being cared for and invested in? Are you being pastored? Bottom line, are you being loved? Stay away from places that are more focused on what they can get from you than what they can deposit into you!

I often encourage people that if the church they are attending is their *Sent Place*, they must do everything they can to stay connected. It is in your *Sent Place* that you will experience wholeness and the fulfillment of your destiny.

BREAKING FREE FROM YOUR STUFF

This kind of healing and wholeness happens as God begins to set you free from what I call "your stuff." As this process begins, you might be surprised by what kind of attitudes, emotions, and behaviors begin to surface.

For example, someone starts attending a church. At first, they are excited, convinced they have found their *Sent Place*. They can't say enough good things about the pastor. They feel the church community is so genuine and welcoming. The praise and worship are on point.

But, as time passes, their enthusiasm dwindles. Suddenly, small offenses turn into bigger ones. Every little thing starts to bother them and feels like a major issue. Maybe they're frustrated because others keep taking their favorite seat. Or the worship director won't let them sing on the team. Maybe their connect group leader forgot to call them back.

At this point, they shift their focus onto everyone else's faults, believing it's everyone else's responsibility to make things better for them.

This is exactly when spiritual authority must step in and ask, "What is God trying to teach you? What is He trying to break in you?" Instead of remaining offended and hurt, let's choose to get healed!

They may need a reminder that, often in our *Sent Place*, God will allow irritants to rise to the surface—exposing our "stuff." When God places us where we're supposed to be, we must be willing to stay there—just like the blind man who was sent to the Pool of Siloam (his *Sent Place*).

It's in that place where healing and wholeness are found!

REPEAT OFFENDERS

On the verge of obtaining freedom, many people allow their offenses to drive them from the pool of healing. In these cases, they often come out worse than when they went in. Figuratively speaking, they are not just blind anymore—their blindness has now been compounded because their irritation has grown into offense.

They become spiritual vagabonds, going from church to church, growing more irritated and causing greater trouble at each place they attend. The cycle repeats itself, worsening with each turn. But here's the key: You may find yourself frustrated at times in your *Sent Place*, but stay planted! In the end, it will be worth it!

Whatever God's *Sent Place* is for you—whether it's a process, a ministry, a church, or a specific role you're called to fulfill—stay there so the work can be completed in you.

It hurts to heal, but at New Beginnings Church, we've worked hard to create an environment where healing doesn't have to be hard. As pastors, we are committed to helping people remain in their *Sent Place* long enough to wash in the pool and experience true wholeness.

I pray that if you haven't already found a church like that, you soon will!

STEPS TO A MIRACLE

In John 9:11, when the blind man was asked what happened to him, he simply shared the steps to his miracle: "A Man called Jesus made clay and anointed my eyes and said to me, 'Go to the pool of Siloam and wash.' So I went and washed, and I received sight."

He went, he washed, and he received. You cannot receive your miracle without the first two steps. The blind man obeyed Jesus' instruction, going to his *Sent Place*. And when he arrived, he washed.

We don't know how long this process took, but it required time and obedience. Sometimes your own process may feel like it's taking forever—like there's no end in sight. Anxiously, you wait, but the process continues, bringing even greater discomfort. Then, finally, the Holy Spirit reveals the root of your dysfunction. You repent, healing comes, and your process is complete.

Have you ever had a moment like that? I certainly have. God will often reveal the root of our problem in the midst of our discomfort—right in the middle of the fire.

Free in the Fire

During our family's eighteen-year battle, one of the most profound lessons we learned came from Daniel 3. King Nebuchadnezzar ordered Shadrach, Meshach, and Abednego to be thrown into the fiery furnace for refusing to bow before the golden image he made. Bound hand and foot, they were cast into the fire.

Now, it's easy to get excited about the best part of this story—when Jesus, the fourth man, appeared in the fire! However, I believe it is just as important to focus on what those three men were doing when the fourth man showed up. Nebuchadnezzar looked into the furnace and saw not just three men, but four, and he declared, "'Look!...I see four men loose, walking in the midst of the fire; and they are not hurt, and the form of the fourth is like the Son of God'" (Dan. 3:25). They were walking around, unbound and unharmed! They were thrown in bound, but while in the fire, they became free (Dan. 3:24–25).

> YOU WILL NEVER BE FREE *FROM* YOUR FIRE UNTIL YOU GET FREE *IN* YOUR FIRE.

We need to adjust our prayer focus. We often pray, "God, deliver me *from* this fire!" But instead, we should ask, "God, what are You trying to set me free from while I'm *in* the fire?"

As I've learned through my own experience, you will never be free *from* your fire until you get free *in* your fire.

Stay in your appointed place—even if it's hot—until freedom has come. Wash until you receive your sight.

Stay Where You're Sent

CHANGED IN A MOMENT

After the blind man at the pool of Siloam washed, Scripture says he "came back seeing" (John 9:7). Imagine the confusion that arose in the neighborhood as he came back, walking home by himself, fully able to see. The people questioned among themselves, "Isn't this the blind man who sat and begged? He looks a lot like that guy...but it can't be him, can it?" (paraphrased from John 9:8–9).

In John 9:9 we are told one individual declared, "Yes, it's him," while another argued, "No, it can't be. It must be someone who resembles him." Then the once-blind man spoke up to settle the controversy. Imagine their shock when he boldly declared, "I am he."

This man was changed in a moment! He went from blindness to sight. He was so miraculously transformed that he became unrecognizable, even to those who had known him best.

> He answered and said, "A Man called Jesus made clay and anointed my eyes and said to me, 'Go to the pool of Siloam and wash.' So I went and washed, and I received sight."
>
> —JOHN 9:11

When God removes the "dys" from your "function," you will be so healed, so free, and so changed that even those who have known you your whole life will barely recognize you.

I'm talking about receiving such a radical work of healing that people will look at you and say, "Looks like them, smells like them, and smiles like them...but is that really them?"

I'm talking about healing so profound that it dramatically changes how you think, feel, and behave. For example, I've seen people who were once introverted, withdrawn, and reclusive due to past wounds experience a moment of divine healing—and suddenly, they smile from ear to ear, unafraid, and begin to reconnect with people again.

Those who have known them their whole lives are baffled, wondering, "What happened? They are so different, so free. Is that really them?"

Yes, I'm talking about being so completely healed that people do a double take and ask, "What happened?"

The redemptive work of the cross creates a "new you." Once you accept Christ, there should be an immediate change in your identity, your actions, and even your associations (whom you surround yourself with). But the work of redemption doesn't end there.

There is a lifelong process of sanctification that begins the moment we surrender to Christ and continues daily. Every day, we should become more like Him.

Think about how completely transformed the blind man was after he was healed. His identity changed—he went from being the blind man to the healed man. He went from begging for his provision to being able to work and provide for himself. His entire countenance changed. Everything about him was different. So different, in fact, that he became unrecognizable to those around him.

Refusing to See

Transformation is an incredible thing! When your life has been truly transformed, you naturally want everyone to know it and celebrate what God has done. But the sad reality is, some people will never see, recognize, or even acknowledge the work of God in your life.

This was the case in John 9:18. After the eyes of the blind man were opened, the Pharisees, blinded by their own disbelief, began asking the man's parents one hard question after another, demanding to know how this miracle took place. Yet no matter what was said, they refused to believe it. Ironically, they had now become the ones with a "seeing" problem.

They interrogated the blind man's parents, but they didn't believe their account. Finally, they questioned the blind man himself, and when he said, "I have already told you. This man put clay on my eyes, I washed, and now I see" (paraphrased from John 9:27), they refused to believe this miracle came from God!

No matter how many times you tell certain people about the transformation in your life, they will still refuse to "see."

The Pharisees were the religious leaders of the day, and as such, they were quick to accuse whoever performed this miracle of not being from God. After all, in their minds, Jesus had sinned by healing the blind man on the Sabbath.

You see, religion has a problem with sovereign power. It demands that everything happen a certain way, following a specific set of rules. The Pharisees were no different. They had "...a form of godliness but [denied] its power" (2 Tim. 3:5). Their religion placed limits on God's power. But the truth is, His miracle-working power cannot be confined to a set of human rules.

Our God is sovereign, almighty, and all-powerful! He is not just someone we call on in times of trouble—He is the Deliverer, the Healer! He can't be explained, and He certainly can't be confined by "religion."

"Religion" will usually try to talk you out of your sovereign experience. Isn't that what the Pharisees tried to do with the blind man who was healed? Thankfully, he refused to deny his experience, boldly declaring, "I don't know what happened to me—all I know is that I was once blind, and now I see."

When God's sovereign power touches lives, you will often hear testimonies like "I don't know what happened to me. I can't explain it. All I know is I was once bound by fear, but now I have courage." Or, "I used to be insecure, but now I'm confident, and I know who I am in Christ. I can't tell you how it happened—I just know it did!"

Even in the face of undeniable evidence, the Pharisees still refused to believe the blind man's testimony. "But the Jews did not believe concerning him, that he had been blind and received his sight..." (John 9:18). They challenged the validity of his miracle, unwilling to accept what was right before their eyes.

FAMILY SECRETS

Nobody knows your "stuff" better than your own family. Remember, when the Pharisees refused to believe that the blind man had received his sight, they called his parents. Why? Because nobody knows you like your family does. You can fool your friends, coworkers, and even your pastor, who may only know the edited version of you. But your family? They see the raw, unedited version.

It's human nature to put on our best behavior in public, and as Christians, we try to hold ourselves to an even higher standard when we're at church. However, for some, the ride home on Sundays might sound like this: "Nice to see you brought your good attitude to church today. But man, you are a hypocrite. If only they could see how you acted yesterday."

Nobody knows you like your family does. They eat with you. Some sleep under the same roof as you. They watch you pray—and then they see you lose your temper when you're angry. They see the good, the bad, the ugly, and the even uglier.

As much as we like to believe that the edited version of us is who we really are, the truth is that the person you are at home is the real you. Your family will be the first to recognize when a sovereign work has taken place in your life because they know the real you. They are the ones who will affirm that you've been healed from your dysfunction. Often God will use this as confirmation of your transformation. Obviously, dysfunctional people may not be able to fully recognize the work God has done, but even they will notice there's a difference.

Unfortunately, far too many people have mastered the art of the "church mask." It's as if they paint it on their face right before they turn into the church parking lot. They can fool many—but not their family.

Like any pastor, I love meeting with people after service and hearing that a sermon really spoke to them. It makes my heart happy when people acknowledge the gift God has given me and receive from it.

As much as those things mean to me, they pale compared to when those closest to me—my wife, my kids, or my parents—say something that acknowledges my growth. I know that if the people who see me in my everyday life recognize a positive change, then they're seeing the real me.

If my wife says, "You're a man of integrity," then that means the real me is a man of integrity. If my parents say, "Jonathan, we're proud of the man you've become," then they're talking about the man they see daily—the way I treat my wife, how I respond as a husband, how I handle my finances, how I deal with pressure, and more.

Their affirmation reminds me that even though I still have areas that need improvement, I'm making it!

Beginning the Process

I truly believe in the delivering power of God Almighty. He is mighty to deliver, and His deliverance brings immediate results. But healing often involves a process that takes time. The kind of healing I'm referring to rarely happens as a one-and-done encounter or a single prayer. It's a process, and that process takes time.

When you're seven or eight years old and something wounds you deeply, you don't yet have the maturity to handle that kind of wound, either intellectually or emotionally. If your parents don't know how to minister healing to you and fail to properly address the wound, you could grow into a sixty-year-old person who has never matured past the age of seven in certain areas of your psyche and emotions.

I've seen many grown men trapped emotionally—twelve-year-olds living inside forty- or fifty-year-old bodies—because, emotionally, we often stop developing at the point of our deepest wounds.

So what does God do? He takes us all the way back. Age five, seven, twelve, twenty-five, thirty-five—wherever that wound first occurred. You've got to return to that place to deal with the injury that you've spent years ignoring and denying.

And that's where the real battle begins.

When this process starts, the natural tendency is to pull away, shut down, or run. Confronting our wounds hurts. But if you truly want healing, you've got to let Him open the wound, take the brush, and scrub out the infection.

If you allow God to take you through this process properly—without resisting or rushing—it will hurt... but He will heal.

Prayer

Father, I give You all the wounds of my past. Open them up and bring healing to my life. Help me to surrender the hurt and the pain of my past to You, so that You can turn my tragedies into trophies. Heal my past, remove dysfunction, transform me, and make me completely whole—spirit, soul, and body. Amen.

Chapter 9

YOU ARE CALLED TO LEAD

As representatives of Jesus, when we are made whole, we bear the responsibility of bringing that wholeness to others. No matter what your title, position, or place in life, there are people you influence. That, in itself, makes you a leader.

Great leaders do not become great by guessing or speculating. They set themselves apart by building on their experiences—whether successes or failures. I encourage you to use your experiences to lead others to the same wholeness you are finding. As leaders, we cannot take anyone somewhere we have not been ourselves. We must be healed before we can lead others into healing. And as you experience wholeness, you will naturally lead others to theirs.

An example of this principle can be seen in the account of Moses and the twelve men who were sent into the land of Canaan. Numbers 13 shows that Moses gave very specific instructions to these men—when to go, where

> WE MUST BE HEALED BEFORE WE CAN LEAD OTHERS INTO HEALING.

to go, and what information to gather and report back. Some of these instructions included reporting how many people were present, whether they were strong or weak, what type of structure they lived in (tents or strongholds), whether the land was good or bad, and if there was wood, as well as bringing back fruit from the first season.

Perhaps the most important instruction of all was to ensure that, no matter what they encountered, they would view it through the eyes of courage.

As the story progresses, we see that of the twelve men sent into Canaan, only Joshua and Caleb were filled with courage and unwavering faith as they shared their report of the land. "Let us go up at once and take possession, for we are well able to overcome it" (Num. 13:30).

Although Moses was the one to instruct the men, it was Joshua who would end up leading the children of Israel into Canaan. Why? Because Joshua had been there before. Joshua was able to lead with boldness and confidence because of his experience.

Your Calling as a Leader

When you think of a leader, what comes to mind? Most of us think of a boss, a commander, or someone "in charge." But a leader is not just someone "in charge." A leader is someone who influences, coaches, inspires, or guides others. Whether you realize it or not, you lead in some capacity every day.

You are not called to just be a seat-filling, song-singing, offering-giving Christian. Regardless of your title, position, economic status, or how long you've followed Christ, you are called by God to lead others to Him. This leadership role comes with a level of responsibility. Like Joshua, you should lead others boldly and confidently into the "land" you have come to know and possess through your personal experiences.

You cannot teach someone to swim if you don't know how to swim yourself. You may be able to explain the mechanics or theory—how to take a breath, let the body float, and kick the legs—but you cannot demonstrate swimming for them. And if you can't demonstrate it, how can you confidently convince them they can do it?

As we saw with Joshua, you cannot lead anyone anywhere you haven't gone yourself. Put another way, you cannot lead anyone into a level of healing you have not personally experienced.

> YOU CANNOT TEACH SOMEONE TO SWIM IF YOU DON'T KNOW HOW TO SWIM YOURSELF.

For example, how can you guide someone into a place of security and confidence in Christ if you haven't first experienced it for yourself?

Jesus taught this principle when He compared the Pharisees to blind men in their attempt to lead others to God. The Pharisees attempted to lead by rules and rituals. They could not guide God's people into a relationship with Him because they did not have one themselves. Their intentions may have been good. However, they could not teach what they did not know. It was not enough to provide the leadership the people needed.

Let them alone. They are blind leaders of the blind. And if the blind leads the blind, both will fall into a ditch.
—MATTHEW 15:14

And He spoke a parable to them: "Can the blind lead the blind? Will they not both fall into the ditch?"
—LUKE 6:39

Using this example as it relates to healing, I must ask a question and point out the obvious: How can co-dependent people lead other co-dependent people without both ending up in the ditch of co-dependency? Dysfunctional leaders cannot lead dysfunctional people without reproducing more dysfunction. It doesn't matter how talented or gifted the leader may be—the outcome will still be failure.

LEAD FROM A PLACE OF WHOLENESS

True leadership begins with transformation. You cannot give what you do not have, and you cannot lead where you have not been. Healing is not just for you—it's for those you are called to lead, guide, and influence. Your personal journey of healing is the foundation that will empower you to lead others with confidence and authenticity. As Joshua could lead with boldness because he had already stepped into the land of promise, you, too, are called to step into healing so you can lead others into their own freedom.

It is time to stop allowing past wounds and insecurities to dictate your effectiveness as a leader. The world doesn't need more blind guides—it needs leaders who have been refined, restored, and made whole in the presence of God. Choose healing. Choose wholeness. Step boldly into your calling as a leader, and as you do, watch how God uses your transformation to bring others into His promise.

Prayer

Lord, I accept my role as a leader. But I ask that I would be a healed leader who leads from a place of wholeness. I pray that as You help me discover healing in my life, I will then be able to inspire and lead others to theirs. In Jesus' name, amen.

Chapter 10

THE PROCESS

THROUGHOUT THIS BOOK, we've examined Naaman's journey—the great commander marked for greatness yet burdened with leprosy. We've explored his status, his struggles, and the moment he stood at the threshold of his breakthrough. But before Naaman could receive his healing, he had to embrace something most of us resist: the process.

How many times have we expected an instant fix to a lifelong issue? We want deliverance without discomfort. We want freedom without submission. We want healing on our terms. But God rarely works that way.

Naaman's healing wasn't about dipping in a river—it was about obedience, humility, and surrender to God's process. In this chapter, we'll look at how his reaction mirrors our own resistance to God's instructions and how breakthrough comes only when we yield to the process.

> But Naaman became furious, and went away and said, "Indeed, I said to myself, 'He will surely come out to me, and stand and call on the name of the

LORD his God, and wave his hand over the place, and heal the leprosy.'"

—2 KINGS 5:11

As we've discussed, Naaman—a man once marked for greatness—now stands at the prophet Elisha's door, disfigured and weakened. His body is being ravaged by leprous sores. Suddenly, all his successes seem meaningless as he finds himself not defending his king but fighting for his own life.

Naaman had heard firsthand the testimonies of healing and restoration from the servant girl. Can you imagine the anticipation he must have felt as he waited for the prophet to open the door and grant him healing instantly?

As footsteps approached and the door cracked open, a smile likely spread across Naaman's face. His heart raced as his mind shouted, "Freedom is here!" He prepared himself to greet the prophet and receive his miracle.

But when the door fully opened, it wasn't the great prophet Elisha who stood before him—but a messenger. Stunned, Naaman blurted out, "Who are you?"

The messenger responded, "I have been sent by the prophet with a message for you."

Naaman stammered, "There must be some mistake. I had an appointment with the prophet, the man of God."

The messenger replied, "Well, I am his messenger, and I have been sent here with instructions for you."

Picture the moment. This high-ranking commander—a man of influence, authority, and status—expected to meet with the great prophet himself. He had anticipated that Elisha would personally greet him and grant him

The Process

his miracle. Instead, he was met by a messenger who handed him a list of instructions.

Insulted, Naaman turned around and left, muttering to himself as he walked away in disbelief. "Doesn't this prophet Elisha know who I am? I can't believe this so-called prophet didn't even bother to come out, call on the name of the Lord his God, wave his hand over me, and heal my leprosy!"

His anger escalated. "And then to suggest that I go and wash in the Jordan? That filthy river? Why not one of the rivers of Damascus, which are far superior to all the waters of Israel? There's no comparison! If I must wash in a river, why can't I choose the river myself?" Outraged, Naaman walked away fuming. Instructions have a way of bringing out the rebellion in us.

Today, this story might unfold like this: A church member schedules an appointment with the senior pastor, or an employee has an appointment with the vice president of a company to discuss a pressing concern. This person expects a personal meeting—a handshake, a warm greeting, perhaps even a cup of coffee—followed by immediate answers to their problem.

Instead, when they arrive, an assistant meets them at the door. The assistant hands them a list of instructions and offers a brief farewell: "Hey! Here are your instructions. Have a great day. Thanks."

> **INSTRUCTIONS HAVE A WAY OF BRINGING OUT THE REBELLION IN US.**

Can you imagine? How would that make you feel?

It would be understandable to feel slighted—as if they

didn't deserve this kind of dismissal. Instead of receiving an instant solution, they were simply given a list of tasks.

Naaman's reaction reflects our own human nature. When given instructions rather than an instant solution, we often respond with frustration. We want results without the process.

Processes have a way of exposing our pride. The servant conveyed Elisha's instructions plainly:

> Go and wash in the Jordan seven times, and your flesh shall be restored to you, and you shall be clean.
> —2 Kings 5:10

But instead of embracing the prophet's words, Naaman let his pride cloud his judgment. He rejected the very instructions that held his healing.

Yet time and time again, healing is directly linked to obedience. When we refuse to follow God's process, we often delay the very breakthrough we desperately seek.

Steps in the Process

Instructions in the process of healing often come through godly counsel. That counsel is often in the form of a pastor, counselor, coach, or mentor. It can come from anyone who has been given a place of spiritual authority to speak into your life.

There have been times when those in authority over me have given me instructions that did not make sense to me. I may have received direction to separate myself from certain relationships, change behaviors, or adjust my thought processes. At the time, my mind resisted. I would think, "Something must be wrong with them."

The Process

Over time, however, I have realized that God is not looking for our understanding—He is looking for our willingness to obey. We will eventually come to understand the reasons, but until that time, we must simply trust and obey.

Spiritual covering is a necessity, and there is safety in submitting to spiritual authority.

> Obey those who rule over you, and be submissive, for they watch out for your souls, as those who must give account. Let them do so with joy and not with grief, for that would be unprofitable for you.
> —HEBREWS 13:17

God sends spiritual authority in our lives to help us. Those in leadership are outside of the struggle and can see things that we cannot see for ourselves. Have you ever found yourself in the middle of a bad situation, struggling to see things clearly?

Painful emotions, past experiences, or other struggles may have clouded your view. This is why, even when we do not understand, God directs us through spiritual authority. Instead of exhausting ourselves asking, "Why?" we must recognize our healing, blessing, and breakthrough are contingent upon our obedience, not our understanding.

Look again at Naaman's story.

Naaman was a disciplined military leader, a man of self-control. Yet in this account, Naaman was furious. In fact, he was so enraged he did not even respond to Elisha's messenger. Instead, he turned and walked away grumbling. Scripture tells us:

> But Naaman became furious, and went away and said, "Indeed, I said to myself, 'He will surely come out to me, and stand and call on the name of the LORD his God, and wave his hand over the place, and heal the leprosy.'"
> —2 KINGS 5:11

Naaman *thought* his healing would happen a certain way—and when it didn't, he struggled to accept the process.

In other words, Naaman was saying, "I *thought* I could dictate the terms of my process. I *thought* I could decide how long I'd be in it, what steps I would take, and how quickly I would get out of it."

Here is the problem: He *thought*. Healing does not come through human reasoning, so we cannot allow our minds to interfere with the process.

This applies to you and me. We must discard all the "I thoughts."

- "I thought it would be this way or that way."
- "This is not what I imagined or how I pictured this would go."

Many of us, like Naaman, believe our healing process should be quick and simple. Make no mistake—I fully believe in miracles and the instantaneous power of God. I have seen people healed instantaneously of various diseases and conditions. However, when it comes to inner healing, it usually takes time. It's a process.

We do not get to decide the process. We do not get to

dictate the steps. We do not get to determine the timeline. We are not in charge.

Our role? Wait for instructions. Obey the process.

Had it not been for Naaman's servants overhearing the instructions and being brave enough to speak up, Naaman might have abandoned the process altogether. The servants offered this advice to Naaman:

> And his servants came near and spoke to him, and said, "My father, if the prophet had told you to do something great, would you not have done it? How much more than when he says to you, 'Wash and be clean'?"
>
> —2 KINGS 5:13

Finally, Naaman did as Elisha directed. He made his way to the Jordan River and dipped seven times.

> So he went down and dipped seven times in the Jordan, according to the saying of the man of God; and his flesh was restored like the flesh of a little child, and he was clean.
>
> —2 KINGS 5:14

Naaman's healing process almost ended prematurely because of his own expectations.

I believe the first step in the process is a willingness to surrender—no matter what it takes to be healed. So many people never find their healing because they refuse to go through the process. They lack the "want-to." They refuse to give up control of their life. They refuse to be obedient.

And in the end, they end up choosing bondage over freedom.

Choosing bondage over freedom probably seems like a ridiculous concept. Why would anybody willingly choose bondage over freedom? Yet I see this happen all the time.

Why? Because bondage is familiar.

For many, it's all they have ever known, and over time, they become comfortable in their captivity. Some have been bound for so long that they don't even realize they are still in bondage.

A Captive Mindset

A powerful example of this can be found in the story of the children of Israel during their exodus from Egypt.

For years, they were enslaved by the Egyptians, suffering under oppression and hardship. They lived in poverty, receiving just enough food to sustain them so they could continue their labor. But when their deliverer, Moses, led them out of Egypt, something surprising happened. Even though they had longed for freedom, they quickly became uncomfortable.

You might wonder—how can freedom be uncomfortable? As the Israelites faced challenges in the wilderness, they began to long for the very life they had been desperate to escape. They grumbled against Moses, wanting the predictability of Egypt instead.

> And the children of Israel said to them, "Oh, that we had died by the hand of the LORD in the land of Egypt, when we sat by the pots of meat and when we ate bread to the full! For you have brought us

out into this wilderness to kill this whole assembly with hunger."

—Exodus 16:3

Though God provided for them—manna to eat daily, a cloud by day, and a fire by night to guide them (Exod. 13:21–22, 16:4–5)—their captivity mindset kept them from embracing their freedom. Even though they were no longer slaves, they still lived as though they were. Their limited, victimized perspective prevented them from recognizing God's security and provision.

Walking in freedom is not always easy.

Like the children of Israel, when we face unfamiliar challenges, we may find ourselves longing for the struggles of the past—simply because they were familiar. This is seen in an extreme way when someone leaves a physically abusive relationship, only to return to it. Though they don't want to be abused, the unknown aspects of freedom can feel overwhelming. They have learned how to dysfunction. They know what to expect. They have developed coping mechanisms. It may be painful, it may be destructive, but it's familiar. And for many, the comfort of the familiar can feel safer than the challenges of freedom.

> Stand fast therefore in the liberty by which Christ has made us free, and do not be entangled again with a yoke of bondage.
>
> —Galatians 5:1

Submit to the Process

Naaman nearly missed his healing because it didn't come the way he expected. How often do we resist God's process because it challenges our pride or feels unfamiliar? Like the Israelites longing for Egypt, many choose the comfort of bondage over the uncertainty of freedom.

Healing requires surrender. Will you trust God's way, even when it's not what you envisioned? The next chapter will help you recognize the mindset shifts needed to fully embrace your freedom. You weren't meant to stay stuck—you were meant to be whole.

> **How often do we resist God's process because it challenges our pride or feels unfamiliar?**

Prayer

Dear Jesus, help me in my process. I need patience. I need humility. I need to submit. Give me the faith and trust needed to submit to instruction. I will not allow the enemy to bring me back to old mindsets. Walking in freedom may not be easy, but Your grace is sufficient. Amen.

Chapter 11

SURRENDERING TO THE PROCESS

THE FIRST STEP in addressing any issue is acknowledging that an issue exists. This is integrity. Integrity requires courage. There must be recognition of the need and then the willingness to embark on the journey toward wholeness.

Naaman saw his issue. He recognized that his problem was bigger than him. He knew he needed God, which is why he sought out the prophet.

The second step in the process is a willingness to go through it. Often, the process is not what we expect or think it should be, and we must be willing to abandon our preconceived ideas. Naaman had to humble himself, let go of his own expectations, and follow the prophet's instructions. Humbling himself meant surrendering. Eventually and wisely, Naaman chose to surrender his will to the process of healing.

> God resists the proud, but gives grace to the humble.
> —JAMES 4:6

HEALING HURTS

When studying the process of Naaman's healing, I discovered different perspectives on how long it took. Some suggest that Naaman dipped in the river seven times in a row. Others propose that he dipped once a day for seven days. The key, however, is not how long it took but that the process was the same—his healing required him to dip seven times.

This great military leader had to surrender himself and travel to the place he was sent. He could not choose any river. He had to go to the Jordan River, the specific place God had appointed for his healing. He had to obey the instructions, step into the filthy water, and dip seven times.

I can only imagine what went through Naaman's mind each time he submerged himself. Perhaps after the first dip, he came up wiping the muddy water from his diseased limbs, searching for signs of change. Maybe he inspected his skin after the second and third dips, looking for fading spots or relief from pain. Yet no matter what he saw—or didn't see—he had to continue dipping. The process had to be completed before healing was fully realized.

> So he went down and dipped seven times in the Jordan, according to the saying of the man of God; and his flesh was restored like the flesh of a little child, and he was clean.
> —2 KINGS 5:14

WHAT'S IN THE "DIP"?

Let's compare the stories of the blind man at the Pool of Siloam and Naaman. These accounts reveal two key principles: First, where you "dip" is just as important as how many times you "dip." Second, God does not operate within the boundaries of our human logic.

In the story of the blind man at the Pool of Siloam, Jesus spat on the ground, made mud with His saliva, and spread it on the blind man's eyes. Then He told him to go wash in the Pool of Siloam, his *Sent Place*.

> And He said to him, "Go, wash in the pool of Siloam" (which is translated, Sent). So he went and washed, and came back seeing.
> —JOHN 9:7

Similarly, in Naaman's story, Elisha instructed him to go to the Jordan River and dip seven times. The Jordan River was Naaman's *Sent Place*.

Had the blind man refused to go to the Pool of Siloam to wash, or Naaman ignored the instruction to go to the Jordan River, neither one would have received their healing. Their healing was fully manifested only in their *Sent Place*.

Logically, or from a natural perspective, rubbing mud in a blind man's eyes would seem to worsen his condition rather than heal it. Likewise, for someone suffering from diseased limbs and open sores, stepping into a murky, dirty river would seem more likely to introduce new infections than to cleanse and heal. Yet in both cases, God used what appeared to be harmful—mud and filthy water—to bring complete healing.

These stories emphasize the critical importance of recognizing your *Sent Place* and understanding that your healing process may defy what you believe is logical.

Healing is fully realized only in your *Sent Place*, where obedience and faith intersect—even when the process defies logic. It takes very little faith or obedience to do what seems reasonable.

Your *Sent Place* and your process will require you to confront your "dirt"—the hidden wounds, insecurities, and brokenness—before healing is complete. Remember, healing is not found in comfort but in discomfort.

This kind of deep inner healing leaves no room for doubt in God's restorative power. Naaman, who previously honored the gods of Syria, acknowledged not only that the God of Israel is real, but that He alone is God.

THE DANGERS OF DYSFUNCTION

We often assume that leadership is reserved only for those who have a title. However, the truth is, everyone leads someone in some way. You may not be a "boss," but you are still a leader.

Leaders influence those around them, and when a leader is dysfunctional in any area, that dysfunction will inevitably impact others. Whether their influence is significant or minimal, a leader struggling with dysfunction will have an adverse effect on those they lead.

In the same way that Naaman's leprosy was contagious and capable of spreading to anyone he encountered, a dysfunctional leader struggling with insecurity and fear will also affect and infect those around them. Regardless of the specific dysfunction, every dysfunction carries its own dangers. Naaman's story powerfully illustrates the dangers of dysfunction.

Imagine for a moment how overwhelmed with joy

Surrendering to the Process

Naaman must have been when his leprosy was cleansed. In that instant, everything in Naaman's life was restored. Made whole, he was no longer the social outcast he had once been. With his dysfunction gone, he could return to his military career and the life he had previously enjoyed. He was healed and miraculously made whole.

Dysfunction brings loss, grief, and destruction, but when you allow God to remove the "dys" from your "function," everything changes.

It's heartbreaking to witness individuals marked for greatness—full of tremendous potential, unique gifts, and powerful callings—being derailed by attacks that target their weakness and unaddressed dysfunctions. These attacks can lead to moral failures, addictions, emotional crises, broken marriages, and blatant sin.

> DYSFUNCTION BRINGS LOSS, GRIEF, AND DESTRUCTION, BUT WHEN YOU ALLOW GOD TO REMOVE THE "DYS" FROM YOUR "FUNCTION," EVERYTHING CHANGES.

If we examine Naaman's story more closely, we see the subtle ways dysfunction takes root and the devastating impact it can have on a person's life.

DECEPTION OR DESTINY

After Naaman was healed, he repeatedly attempted to bestow gifts upon Elisha as a token of gratitude. Naaman offered silver and garments to Elisha, but each time, his offer was rejected. After several failed attempts, Naaman finally gave up and prepared to leave.

Naaman and his servants gathered the gifts offered to Elisha and headed down the road, rejoicing over what had just occurred in the Jordan.

As Naaman and his company faded into the distance, Gehazi, the servant of Elisha, began to think about what had just transpired. At that moment, I believe his next actions revealed the deceit that had been lurking in his heart.

> But Gehazi, the servant of Elisha the man of God, said, "Look, my master has spared Naaman this Syrian, while not receiving from his hands what he brought; but as the LORD lives, I will run after him and take something from him."
>
> —2 KINGS 5:20

Rather than honoring Elisha's decision to accept nothing from Naaman, Gehazi chose deception. He took off running after Naaman as fast as he could. When Naaman saw him approaching, Scripture says that Naaman "got down from the chariot to meet him, and said, 'Is all well?'" (2 Kings 5:21).

Probably gasping for breath, Gehazi managed to say, "All is well. My master has sent me, saying, 'Indeed, just now two young men of the sons of the prophets have come to me from the mountains of Ephraim. Please give them a talent of silver and two changes of garments'" (2 Kings 5:22).

Naaman had no reason to doubt Gehazi's story and responded by offering even more than was requested. In

Surrendering to the Process

fact, Naaman was so generous that he gave Gehazi an abundance of silver and so many garments that it took two of Naaman's servants to carry everything!

Hoping to slip in unnoticed, Gehazi returned to Elisha. As soon as Elisha saw him, the prophet asked, "Where did you go, Gehazi?" (2 Kings 5:25).

Perhaps forgetting his master was a prophet, Gehazi attempted to cover his tracks. He lied outright, saying, "Your servant did not go anywhere" (2 Kings 5:25). However, the prophet Elisha saw right through Gehazi's words. Without hesitation, Elisha's prophetic gift activated, and he responded sternly:

> Did not my heart go with you when the man turned back from his chariot to meet you? Is it time to receive money and to receive clothing, olive groves and vineyards, sheep and oxen, male and female servants? Therefore the leprosy of Naaman shall cling to you and your descendants forever.
> —2 Kings 5:26–27

The Bible records Gehazi's tragic fate in the closing words of 2 Kings 5:27: "And he went out from his presence leprous, as white as snow." The dysfunction that had just been lifted from Naaman instantaneously fell as judgment upon Gehazi. Why? Naaman's inability to follow instructions almost kept him leprous. Gehazi's disobedience and deception caused him to become leprous.

The greed and deception in his heart surfaced as he sought to profit from something only God could take credit for. As a result, the very judgment that had been lifted from Naaman was placed upon Gehazi.

Before he could even take another breath, he walked out of Elisha's presence covered in leprosy.

Had Gehazi remained faithful in his service to the prophet Elisha, his life could have continued to be one of health and wholeness. He would have remained in his calling, continuing to minister alongside Elisha as he had for many years. Yet he took a detour, and in an instant, he was cursed with a dysfunction that not only could not be hidden but also would lead to absolute disaster and devastation.

No Quick Fix

While we live in a "we-want-it-now," microwave world, true healing does not come with a quick fix. There are no shortcuts. Being healed and made whole is a process—and that process takes time.

For Naaman, that process involved getting into the dirty waters of the Jordan River. His deliverance happened right there, in the middle of that murky, filthy water.

It is easy to deceive ourselves when everything in life seems to be going great. We pretend the dirt and ugliness do not exist. You are thriving—getting promoted, watching your children excel. It feels like everything is "locked in"—spiritually, personally, and professionally. Everything appears perfect.

> THERE ARE NO SHORTCUTS. BEING HEALED AND MADE WHOLE IS A PROCESS—AND THAT PROCESS TAKES TIME.

Yet it is often in those very moments, when everything

seems secure, that we fail to recognize the lurking dysfunctions in our lives. Then, when life takes a turn and begins to fall apart, we are suddenly forced to face the ugliness that has been tucked away beneath the surface. It is in that place that we cry out to God:

"What must I do? How can I save my marriage? What can I do to rescue my children and family? What can I do to break this cycle? How do I get out of this mess? What is it going to take to put an end to this—once and for all?"

When you begin to ask these kinds of questions, it is a sign that your heart is open. Open to heal. Open to change. Open to take responsibility. Open to forgive. Open to let go. Open to allow God to direct you through the steps of your process.

Lastly and most importantly, you must be open to submit to the process!

Step into the New

Your past may have shaped you, but it does not have to define you. Healing is not just about letting go—it's about stepping into the new. God is calling you to move forward, to break free from the weight of past wounds, and to embrace the fullness of what He has for you. You cannot carry old mindsets, past hurts, or familiar dysfunctions into the new season He has prepared for you. It's time to make a decision: Will you remain stuck in the past, or will you surrender to the process and step into the healing, freedom, and destiny God has ordained for you? The choice is yours. Move forward.

Prayer

Heavenly Father, help me to surrender to the process. Even though at times it may not make sense, I will choose to trust You. My healing is not in what's logical and what makes sense; it is in my obedience. Give me the courage to find my sent place, to stay in my sent place, and to not abandon my sent place until I am made whole. In Jesus' name I pray, amen.

Chapter 12

HEALING

THE REAL WORK of healing begins when we are willing to face our own dirt and ugliness with a heart of integrity. True freedom comes only through truth. "And you shall know the truth, and the truth shall make you free" (John 8:32). Yet, too often, people seek freedom through every means but the truth. But God's word is clear—freedom comes through truth. I like to say it like this: You are only as free as the amount of truth you are willing to embrace.

Maybe you've been dealing with some messes over the last few months or years. Have you stopped to ask, "What is God trying to teach me? What is He trying to show me?" Instead of resisting the process, learn the lesson. Embrace the truth. Transformation will follow.

For Naaman, his process was completed after he dipped seven times in the Jordan. The number seven symbolizes completion. This is first seen in the account of creation itself. On the seventh day, God rested—every aspect of creation was complete (Gen. 2:2). Seven represents something being fulfilled. Through Elisha's instruction to dip seven times, I believe God was telling

Naaman, "I am going to keep you in this process until the work is completed in you."

For example, people who constantly struggle with feelings of rejection will continue to find themselves in situations where rejection occurs—until they learn to overcome it and are no longer affected by rejection. Those who battle insecurity will be repeatedly confronted with situations that trigger those insecurities—until there is nothing left for insecurity to cling to.

You ask, "How will I know when I've overcome insecurity?" You'll know when the very things that used to bother you, frustrate you, and make you angry no longer have power over you.

How do you know when the wound is truly healed? It is healed when someone can poke at it without causing any pain or irritation.

> YOU ARE ONLY AS FREE AS THE AMOUNT OF TRUTH YOU ARE WILLING TO EMBRACE.

I encourage you to stay in your process until the wound no longer hurts—until all the pain of that insecurity is completely gone. When you reach the place where someone can insult you, mock you, or call you names, yet it no longer shakes your identity or emotional state, that's how you'll know you're healed. Sure, it may still irritate you, but it won't cause your entire world to implode.

The process of healing can be long. In some ways, healing is a lifelong journey. You must be committed to the process—because parts of it may last the rest of your life.

Healing takes time. Stay in the process until it is complete.

Some of the very things I now walk in victory over were once some of my greatest struggles. Insecurity is the biggest one that comes to mind. From a young age, I battled deep insecurities—issues that were passed down as generational curses, iniquities that kept me bound for years. But today, I am glad to say that I am walking in victory over those insecurities every single day. And yet I also acknowledge that this victory is something I must continue walking out daily.

Do not be deceived into thinking that you have arrived. Victory requires daily authority. The enemy will always stand at the door, waiting for an opportunity. If you give him even the smallest avenue of access, he'll wedge his foot in the door and try to push his way back in.

You and I can walk in victory over these struggles, but we must never lose awareness that they are our weaknesses.

SEVEN DAYS, SEVEN DIPS

This brings us to the final point regarding the seven days, seven dips. For discussion's sake, let's suppose that Naaman's process required seven days of dipping in the Jordan. Think about this: Each day Naaman would go down into the water and wash. What do you think he saw when he came up after the first dip? Leprosy. Everywhere.

Even though he may have noticed some progress with each dip, the fact remains—until the very last dip, he was not whole. Parts of his fingers and toes were still missing. His flesh was still covered with white rotting sores.

The next day, he went back into the water and dipped again. Maybe, as he came out, he had a smile of expectation on his face. But what did he see?

Leprosy.

A third time he washed and dipped in that dirty water. When he came out, what did he see? Leprosy. Everywhere. Just like the day before.

Can you imagine how Naaman must have felt going back a fourth time? A fifth time? A sixth time? Yet he kept going. He had the courage to continue confronting his condition, facing the same painful reality over and over again.

And then, on the seventh time, as he descended into the muddy waters of the Jordan, something changed. When he came up—he was completely free.

Don't Stop Dipping Until the Process Is Complete

Over the years, I've seen many good people have areas of dysfunction exposed during seasons of fiery trials and great difficulty. Perhaps, during this time, God used someone in authority to speak a word of truth, bringing that problem to light and giving instructions on how to overcome it. In desperation to escape the adversity, they eagerly heed the instruction, hoping for a quick resolution.

However, following the instruction often brings them face-to-face with deep-rooted stuff in their life that they really didn't want to deal with.

Oh yes, at first, they cry and repent, "Lord, I'm sorry. Forgive me. Show me why I'm in this mess. Reveal all the problem areas in my life that need to be healed. Show me how I got to be the way I am and why I do what I do." Then the Lord answers their prayer, and suddenly they are overwhelmed. They never imagined how much junk had been buried inside them.

For years, they were professionals at walking around in deception—blind to their issues of insecurity, fear, abandonment, rejection, and pride. Of course, everyone else saw their struggles, but they didn't. So when God finally opens their eyes, allowing them to "see" themselves for who they really are, their reaction is something like "Man, this is really ugly. It's too much to handle. I can't believe I'm like this."

Have you ever had an experience like this? Naaman did. He had to look at his leprosy day after day and confront it. Symbolically for us, it might sound like "I'm insecure, I have pride, I've been hurt, and I don't bond well with people." Naaman had to face his condition every single day until the process was complete. The same is true for you and for me.

Think of the process of inner emotional healing in comparison to physical healing. Most of us have had, or know someone who has had, surgery to repair an issue. There's a problem that's causing pain or dysfunction, and after ignoring it for too long, the person finally consults a doctor for help.

The doctor says surgery is needed. The operation takes place, uncovering and exposing the root issue. The surgeon repairs the problem and closes the wound. It is at that moment when healing begins.

Yet here's what many don't realize—healing often hurts more than the injury itself.

Let's use the example of a hip replacement. After

the joint is replaced, the healing process takes weeks, even months. The person must endure the pain of standing and putting weight on the new joint. Walking, bending, sitting, standing—it all hurts, initially almost unbearably so. But slowly, as the healing continues, the pain lessens. Daily activities become easier. Eventually, they experience total restoration and freedom from all pain.

Now imagine if they quit the process before healing was complete. If the patient chooses to avoid the pain of recovery, refusing to move or do the necessary physical therapy, they will remain bound—limping through life, still struggling with the very issue the surgery was meant to fix.

Deep inner emotional healing works the same.

The initial wound occurs, but instead of dealing with the pain, we stuff it down, pretending it's not there. Time passes. The injury continues to worsen until the pain or symptoms can no longer be ignored. We seek help. The Great Physician steps in and begins the surgery.

He exposes the root issue and provides instructions for total healing.

But here's the critical moment. As the healing process begins and we feel the pain of the process, we reach a crossroads. Either we press through the pain to total restoration, or we abandon the process and limp through life—forever bound to our pain.

Renewed and Restored

Last but not least—and perhaps the most exciting part of it all—at the end of Naaman's process, he didn't just come out clean. If you think that was the full extent of the miracle, you missed the deeper message.

When Naaman emerged from the waters of the Jordan after dipping seven times, he wasn't just cured of leprosy. Scripture tells us he came out with his flesh like that of a child (2 Kings 5:14).

God doesn't just want to heal you—He wants to restore you. He wants to heal you so deeply, so completely, that He even restores your innocence and purity that dysfunction stole from you.

When a child experiences abuse, it wounds them deeply. It damages their heart, their emotions, and their identity. Those wounds often go unhealed, trapping them in a cycle of insecurity that follows them into adulthood.

As they grow, because those wounds were never properly healed, they begin living a life dominated by insecurity. They find reasons—every single day—to affirm that insecurity. They search for proof that they aren't good enough, that no one likes them, that they will never measure up.

Life is full of moments that try to deepen the unhealed wounds of our past. But the story of Naaman reveals that God's desire isn't just to remove dysfunction—He wants to restore. He wants to heal so completely that there isn't even a trace of the past left behind.

Naaman's leprosy had likely done more than just cover him with sores. The disease may have eaten away at his skin, his fingers, his nose, his hair, and parts of his hands and feet.

Naaman's need for healing went far beyond the

surface. Even if the sores were gone, it's only fair to assume that the damage caused by the horrible disease would have remained.

Yet Scripture tells us Naaman wasn't just healed—he was made whole. God restored him in such a dynamic way that even the scars of his past were erased.

Total restoration was his. His flesh was renewed—soft, unblemished, like that of a child. Every trace of destruction completely gone!

Let the Process Begin

Do you long to experience true freedom—total healing from your dysfunction? Do you want God to heal you so completely that you become unrecognizable to those who have known you for years? Do you want them to look at you and say, "Who are you? You don't even look or sound the same"?

I'm talking about being healed so deeply, so completely, that even those who know you best—your parents, spouse, children, neighbors, coworkers—can't deny something dramatic has happened to you.

The transformation in you will be so profound that words won't be enough to explain it.

> I'M TALKING ABOUT BEING HEALED SO DEEPLY, SO COMPLETELY, THAT EVEN THOSE WHO KNOW YOU BEST—YOUR PARENTS, SPOUSE, CHILDREN, NEIGHBORS, COWORKERS—CAN'T DENY SOMETHING DRAMATIC HAS HAPPENED TO YOU.

Those around you will react just like the parents of the blind man did when questioned about their son. "We know our son. We know he was born blind. How he can see now, we don't know. All we know is that once he was blind, but now he can see" (paraphrased from John 9:20–21).

Something deep within you is stirring. You feel it. You know it. You're saying, "I have the 'want-to.' I want to be healed. I want to be whole. Even if the process is long. Even if it gets ugly at times. I am willing. I am ready."

If that's you, it's time. It's time to sign the waiver.

Give the Master Surgeon permission to do whatever He needs to do.

Pray this prayer with me:

PRAYER

Father, I thank You for this Word. I have identified the necessity of the process. Holy Spirit, I pray that You would give me the strength and courage to be obedient. Grant me the grace I need to keep myself in that Jordan River, that Pool of Siloam, and not move until the process is complete.

Lord, help me to be willing to face my dysfunction—even in the midst of the dirt and ugliness that is not pleasant to look at or acknowledge. Help me confront the things I have allowed to remain in my life. Give me the courage not to take my eyes off them until the process has been completed and I am healed and made whole.

Holy Spirit, I release You to do that work in me. Begin the process starting today, so I can be healed as I am restored and made whole. Amen.

Chapter 13

THE WAY WE SEE

Have you ever struggled with your perception? Have you seen something one way, only to later discover it was completely different? Have you ever felt foolish for believing in a version of reality that was not actually true? I know I have. It's embarrassing to realize how far off our understanding can be from the truth. False perceptions lead us to incorrect conclusions.

There are many reasons our perception can become distorted. Trauma, neglect, abandonment, abuse, family dysfunctions, and generational curses all have a way of altering how we see the world. Often, we see situations, relationships, and even God through the filter of our past. This distorted perspective creates a cycle of false perceptions.

Let's look further into some of these reasons behind distorted perceptions and how they shape the way we see life.

In Mark 8, Jesus visits Bethsaida.

> Then He came to Bethsaida; and they brought a blind man to Him, and begged Him to touch him. So He took the blind man by the hand and led him

out of the town. And when He had spit on his eyes and put His hands on him, He asked him if he saw anything. And he looked up and said, "I see men like trees, walking." Then He put His hands on his eyes again and made him look up. And he was restored and saw everyone clearly.

—MARK 8:22–25

Some biblical studies suggest that in this passage, *tuphlos*, the Greek word for "blind," does not necessarily refer to someone who was completely without sight, but rather to a person whose vision was cloudy or impaired.[1] However, it's clear his vision was significantly hindered because he needed help getting around. No amount of squinting or straining his eyes could bring clarity—his sight was obstructed.

Because of this, Jesus didn't simply say, "Follow Me." Instead, He took the man by the hand and led him out of town. Perhaps he wasn't entirely blind, but the term *blind* remains an accurate description of his condition.

Some scholars suggest that his blindness was not only physical but also spiritual or mental. Physically, his eyesight was impaired. Mentally, his perception may have been clouded by distorted thinking or dysfunction. Regardless, he was in need of a miracle.

I have read this story many times, and each time, it excites me because I love to see how Jesus brings healing and wholeness. As incredible as this miracle was, the most profound aspect is found beneath the surface. When we examine the story more closely, we see just how truly amazing it is. Believe me, there's more to this account than meets the eye.

The Way We See

THE HEALER IS HERE!

The news likely spread like wildfire that Jesus had returned to Bethsaida. Time and again throughout the New Testament, we read how Jesus healed all (Matt. 12:15). Miracles seemed to happen wherever Jesus went.

Yet this miracle stands out because Jesus did something He had never done before. He took the blind man by the hand and led him out of the city. Clearly, Jesus wanted to minister to him in a more intimate setting, away from the crowd. Perhaps this allowed Jesus to build a rapport with the man and strengthen his faith for his miracle. While Scripture doesn't reveal why Jesus chose to do this, it does emphasize the process leading to the miracle.

> So He took the blind man by the hand and led him out of the town. And when He had spit on his eyes and put His hands on him, He asked him if he saw anything. And he looked up and said, "I see men like trees, walking." Then He put His hands on his eyes again and made him look up. And he was restored and saw everyone clearly.
> —MARK 8:23–25

Once outside the town, Jesus spat on the blind man's eyes and laid His hands on him, asking him whether he could see anything. The man responded, "I see men like trees, walking" (Mark 8:24).

Among all the miracles Jesus performed, this is the only recorded instance of a progressive healing. Even though the blind man's reply indicated improvement, the work wasn't yet complete—it had only begun.

While the blind man could now distinguish shapes and movement, his perception remained unclear. Jesus immediately laid His hands on his eyes again and made him look up. Only then was his sight fully restored, allowing him to see with perfect clarity.

Clouded Perceptions

In many accounts of miracles found in Scripture, we are told how long the individual suffered from their condition, particularly if they had been afflicted since birth. But in this instance, we are not given that information. This leads me to believe that something may have happened to him after he was born that caused his issue.

I believe it's entirely possible that he was born with perfect vision, fully able to see things clearly. But, somewhere along the way, something happened that damaged his ability to see, leading to distorted perceptions.

What about you? Do you feel as though you've been viewing life through a haze? Did something happen that impaired your ability to see things clearly?

Most often, clouded perceptions begin at the moment of an emotional or physical injury. Perhaps for you, it started when someone abused you, abandoned you, betrayed you, or deeply hurt you in another way.

Perhaps something occurred in your first marriage that now causes you to look at your current spouse through the distorted lens of your past relationship. Or maybe a negative experience at a previous church has influenced how you perceive every church you've attended since.

The pain inflicted by an injury has a powerful way of skewing our perceptions. In fact, it can completely distort the way we see things. Often, false perceptions develop as a coping mechanism—a subconscious attempt to protect us from further hurt. Yet these same false perceptions can also blind us to the good around us.

The reality is that when someone suffers from false perceptions, they struggle to see anything accurately. Unaddressed pain inevitably spills into present and future relationships. For example, if you've been hurt before, you may find yourself entering new relationships with your guard up, always bracing for betrayal. You find yourself constantly on edge, waiting for that familiar feeling of being stabbed in the back. Hyper-vigilant and overly sensitive, you start searching for signs that someone will eventually do you wrong. You begin living in a defensive posture, anticipating the next wound. Why? Because you are viewing everything through the lens of your past pain.

> THEY CAN CAUSE YOU TO SEE THINGS THAT AREN'T THERE AND BLIND YOU TO WHAT IS.

Unhealed wounds have a way of coloring everything. I can't say it any simpler. They can cause you to see things that aren't there and blind you to what is. Even daily interactions can be distorted. A hurried hello from someone might suddenly feel like a personal affront.

THE REARVIEW MIRROR DRIVER

When you begin to view your present circumstance through the lens of past injuries, it's as if you are trying to drive forward while focusing solely in your rearview mirror!

If you continue to filter your vision through the wounds of your past, not only will your present be distorted, but so will your future. You may know you're seeing something, but you won't be able to perceive it clearly or accurately.

Soon these distortions begin to torment you with doubts and endless questions: questions about everything and everybody.

- "Did they just give me a funny look?"
- "Do they actually like me or not?"
- "What did they really mean when they said that?"
- "Are they for me or against me?"
- "Does the pastor even care about me?"
- "Do I matter to anyone?"
- "Does God really love me?"

If you frequently wrestle with these kinds of thoughts, there's a strong chance you have a distorted perception that needs healing.

The Way We See

ATTENTION PLEASE!

Before the blind man's sight was healed, he had a problem with perception. Imagine what his morning must have been like just hours before his healing took place. First, his friends ushered him out of his house because Jesus had returned to Bethsaida. From within his darkened world, he probably heard his friends excitedly discussing some of the miracles that Jesus had already performed on previous visits.

When they reached Jesus, the blind man heard his friends pleading with Him to touch their companion. I can only imagine the blind man's surprise when Jesus took him by the hand and personally led him out of town. What must have been running through his mind as he walked with Jesus? What did he think when Jesus suddenly stopped, turned toward him, and then—spit in his eyes?

Have you ever wondered about the significance of that moment? There must have been something deeply symbolic about it because Jesus never did anything without a purpose. His actions were never random or without meaning.

I want you to pause for a moment and engage in a simple exercise. Are you ready?

Take your hand and hold it right in front of your mouth. Bring it as close as possible and say, "Thank You, Jesus. Thank You, Jesus. Thank You, Jesus."

Don't whisper. Say it with conviction. "Thank You, Jesus! Thank You, Jesus!"

Now stop and look at your hand. What do you notice? Most likely, it feels damp.

When you speak, your words carry moisture. I believe that when Jesus spit on the blind man's eyes, it was a prophetic act—a symbolic release of His very Word. Because here's the truth: You will never be completely healed without having the Word of God applied to your life.

> Man shall not live on bread alone, but on every word that comes from the mouth of God.
> —MATTHEW 4:4, NIV

The Word of God is so powerful that it can heal every form of blindness in your life. Your perceptions can be restored. Your vision can become clear again. When your distorted perspectives are corrected, you will see yourself—and others—in ways you never imagined possible.

APPLY THE WORD

If you desire to be healed, you must allow the Word of God to be applied directly to the areas of your life where you've been hurt.

We love to apply the Word of God and its promises to our finances, our health, our families, and our relationships. Let's be honest—we love to apply the Word when it aligns with our desires. However, it's far less appealing to apply that same Word to the painful areas of our lives. Rather than surrendering them to healing, we often choose to hide and protect those wounds.

It's easy to sit in church and enthusiastically agree with certain parts of the pastor's sermon. For example, if the pastor is preaching about blessings, favor, great opportunities, and an abundance of open doors, it's easy to shout, "Yes!"

The Way We See

But when the sermon shifts to confronting your own issues, discomfort sets in. You may find yourself fidgeting, scrolling through your phone, and casually checking your social media feeds—refining your skill of "tuning out."

Then, just as you've successfully tuned out the pastor, he shifts back to talking about all the things you love to hear, and suddenly, you're re-engaged!

Don't Tune Out!

As human beings, we have perfected the art of denial, hiding, and covering up our dysfunctions. From an early age, we are taught to conceal our weaknesses. Many have been raised in homes where emotions and feelings were dismissed or suppressed.

So many people struggle with emotional integrity simply because they've never been taught it. They have mastered the art of putting on the right face and maintaining a strong front. They do everything they can to ensure people never see their weaknesses and vulnerabilities. However, true healing begins only when we acknowledge our weaknesses—because it is in our weakness that we can receive Christ's strength.

I encourage you not to tune out. Don't turn away when you hear a truth that convicts you or makes you uncomfortable. Rather, in those moments, lean in. Listen closely to what God is trying to say. Tune in—don't tune out!

The Bible says, "For the word of God is living and powerful, and sharper than any two-edged sword, piercing even to the division of soul and spirit..." (Heb. 4:12). His

Word works! Hear it. Apply it. Be changed by it. The Word will strip away the "dys" so that you can truly "function."

HEALING IS A PROCESS

Remember, the word *healing* speaks of a process—and process takes time. While miracles are instantaneous and creative, healing often requires patience and endurance. It took time for Naaman to dip repeatedly in the Jordan before his leprosy was cleansed. It took time for the blind man in Mark 8 to have his sight restored. Healing is a process—it unfolds over time.

I have found that whenever something requires time, it's easy to grow impatient and want to quit before the process is completed. What if the blind man had said, "You prayed for me once, and it didn't work, so I'm leaving"?

If he had left midway through his process, he would have continued to see "men like trees, walking" (Mark 8:24). He would have experienced improvement, but not complete restoration.

Previously, we discussed another account of a blind man receiving his sight. Jesus spat on the ground, made clay with the spittle, and applied it to the man's eyes. Then He instructed him to wash in the Pool of Siloam. As the blind man obeyed, his sight was restored. But what if he had stopped before completing his process? What if he had said, "This is taking too long. I'm not going to the Pool of Siloam to wash"? What if he had thought, "This clay hurts my eyes—healing shouldn't be painful! I refuse to wait. I'm washing it out now"?

There are clear similarities between these two miracles. Both men faced the same struggle—they were blind. While the process of their healing differed, the end result remained the same. Both were healed as they continued in their processes.

Your healing process may take time. Even though it feels like it's taking too long, don't give up! Wholeness is within reach. Healing may hurt, but it's always worth it.

Don't Settle for Less Than the Best

Perhaps, at times, you have felt as though you've overcome a health issue, conquered a major fear, or experienced emotional healing—only to find that not long afterward, the health issue returns, the fear resurfaces, and emotionally, you feel like a wreck. Does that mean you haven't made any progress? No. Healing is a process. When an issue resurfaces, it's not a sign of failure—it's another opportunity to deal with it on a deeper level. Never allow the enemy to whisper, "It didn't work" or "It's not working." Instead, remain in the process!

Don't settle for less than God's best! It doesn't matter how many times you need to receive prayer. It doesn't matter how often you have to talk about it, acknowledge it, and work through it—stay in the process. Determine to continue until your dysfunction is completely gone. If that means seeking prayer a second, third, or fourth time, then keep pressing in. Keep washing in the Pool of Siloam until your sight is fully restored. Keep dipping in the Jordan River until your leprosy is completely gone.

Stay close to Jesus. Had that blind man not stayed close, he would not have received the second touch that completed his healing. His dysfunction was gone! The Bible says the man "was restored and saw everyone clearly" (Mark 8:25). "Everyone" included Jesus! Don't quit until you see Him clearly!

What Do You See?

At some point in his life, the blind man had apparently seen both trees and people. However, as his eyesight worsened, his vision blurred until everything became indistinguishable.

When Jesus spat in the man's eyes and asked if he could see anything, he could not clearly discern what he was seeing. He saw shapes that looked like trees. But since those shapes were moving, he assumed he was seeing "men like trees, walking" (Mark 8:24). His perception was distorted, preventing him from distinguishing between the two.

How often do we struggle to discern what we see? How often do we fail to differentiate between what is real and what is not? How often do we view life through the lens of past hurts, choosing "our truth" over actual truth?

Distorted perceptions often damage relationships. For example, you form a friendship with someone. They genuinely care for you and treat you with kindness. But because you carry insecurity from past wounds, your perception tells you that no one can be trusted, everyone is out to hurt you, and everybody takes advantage of you. Even though this friend has never mistreated you, you mentally place them in the category of "no one," "everyone," and "everybody." That perception then colors every conversation and interaction you have with them.

Unfortunately, when this happens, we unconsciously create a narrative to validate our false perceptions—even when those perceptions are not based on reality. As long as we hold on to unhealthy perceptions, it is impossible to maintain healthy relationships.

It is dangerous to judge others based on distorted perceptions. We risk losing valuable relationships when we choose our perception of truth over actual truth.

Consider this: Have you ever noticed that three people can hear the same sermon and walk away with completely different opinions about what was said and how it was delivered? One might say, "The message was filled with love and concern." Another might say, "The message was harsh and judgmental." A third might say, "The message rambled and was a waste of time."

Even though all three listened to the same speaker, each heard and perceived something different. Why? Because of their unique perspectives. Likewise, three people can participate in the same conversation yet leave with three different interpretations of what was said. Each one perceives through a different lens.

Perhaps one views life through an optimistic, rose-colored lens. Another sees everything through the lens of insecurity and offense. The third views the world through mistrust and negativity. Differences in perspective are normal and can even be healthy—if those perceptions are not dysfunctional.

The Truth Will Set You Free

If you allow Him, the Holy Spirit will expose areas of dysfunction. When He does, you may not be surprised, as you are somewhat aware of the issue. But there may be other times when His revelation catches you off guard. Why? Because you were previously unaware of its presence in your life.

For example, you may recognize that you tend to see things through the lens of insecurity. But what if you don't realize that this insecurity is rooted in fear—causing you to become controlling and manipulative as a way to protect yourself? When the Holy Spirit begins to peel back the layers, revealing how your insecurity stems from fear and manifests in control and manipulation, you may immediately think, "Oh no. That's not me."

Our natural reaction is to shut down and reject what we don't want to face. After all, who wants to admit they have controlling or manipulative tendencies? Rather than seeing ourselves as we truly are, we often cling to our distorted self-perception because it feels safer and more comfortable.

> You will never experience true healing while focusing on someone else's issues.

Of course, it's always easier to recognize dysfunction in others than to confront our own. Our eyes are wide open to their issues but blind to our own. It's tempting to ignore our dysfunction, pretending it doesn't exist. But

The Way We See

healing begins when we shift our focus inward, allowing God to do His work in us.

> And why do you look at the speck in your brother's eye, but do not perceive the plank in your own eye?
> —Luke 6:41

You will never experience true healing while focusing on someone else's issues. Even though, deep down, we know we have our own struggles, we still tend to see ourselves through rose-colored lenses. We convince ourselves that we aren't really the problem—it's everyone else. If we can blame others, we believe it keeps the focus off us.

But Scripture makes it clear: The Holy Spirit is the revealer of truth.

> But you have an anointing from the Holy One, and you know all things.
> —1 John 2:20

> And you shall know the truth, and the truth shall make you free.
> —John 8:32

The truth about ourselves isn't always easy to hear. Often it hurts. But acknowledging, accepting, and embracing the truth are the keys to your freedom.

Don't Miss Your Miracle

Distorted perceptions, resulting from past injuries, can blind you to the miracles God is placing in your path.

Instead of recognizing a blessing for what it is, you may misinterpret it as a curse. Rather than embracing what God is trying to give you, you reject it—missing out on what He has in store for you.

The reverse is also true. Your flawed perceptions can cause you to mistake a trap from the enemy for a gift from God. Instead of discerning the danger, you embrace it—only to realize too late that what you thought was a blessing was actually a curse. Because your perception isn't trustworthy, you latch on to unhealthy relationships, walk into toxic situations, and find yourself wounded all over again. You trust when you shouldn't, invest when you shouldn't, and ignore warning signs that should have been obvious.

All because a wolf in disguise looked like an innocent sheep.

The enemy thrives on deception, and a distorted perception makes it impossible to see the danger ahead.

Road to Nowhere

Perception issues often lead to self-sabotage, creating a cycle where no matter how hard you try, you keep ending up in the same place—devastation. You seemingly go from one dysfunctional relationship to another. You make choices that seem right at the time, only to later discover they were the wrong decisions. The cycle becomes one of repetitive self-destruction.

Self-destructive cycles come in many forms. Consider these examples:

- Have you ever known someone who jumps from job to job? A great job opportunity comes their way, and they're ecstatic. Yet, within months, they're unemployed again—either quitting or getting fired. This pattern repeats itself with every new job, leaving them stuck in an endless loop of instability.

- What about relationships? One day, a person is madly in love, convinced they've found "the one." The next, they're heartbroken, lamenting how wrong the relationship is. They move on, only to find themself in the same situation over and over again. Each time, they say, "I don't know what happened. This person is just like the one I was with before."

- Then there's the financial roller coaster. Some people seem to fluctuate between seasons of financial abundance and complete lack. One moment, they're flush with cash; the next, they're struggling to get by.

I personally knew someone who appeared to be extraordinarily blessed in finances. They were a "money magnet," constantly attracting financial favor and new opportunities. But every time they reached a place of success, self-sabotage would kick in. Driven by fear and dysfunction, they would make a series of poor decisions—inevitably ending up right back where they started.

Recurring self-destructive cycles can become so ingrained that you accept them as your reality. You convince yourself, "This is just how my life is." But the truth is, you don't have to stay stuck. You don't have to remain captive. These repetitive cycles can be broken—but it takes courage.

The first step? Asking the all-important question: What is the root of my problem?

If you're willing to dig deep and confront the root, you can finally get off the road to nowhere.

Prayer

Heavenly Father, I ask for health in the area of my perceptions. I do not want to see through the filter of past hurt and experiences. I want Your Word to be my filter. I pray that as I continue to apply Your Word to every area of my life, it will continue to bring health and freedom to every area of my life. In Jesus' name, amen.

Chapter 14

SABOTAGE

WHILE SELF-SABOTAGE IS often subtle, it ultimately undermines, disrupts, and destroys. Unless we identify the root cause of our struggles, we will continue sabotaging our own lives and remain stuck on the road to nowhere.

When searching for the real issue, we tend to focus on the most obvious symptoms. For example, if we have financial struggles, we assume the problem is a lack of money. If we experience relationship issues, we believe the solution is finding the right person. If we struggle with emotional pain, we think, "If the hurt would stop, I'd be okay." These are surface-level assessments. But the real problem isn't at the surface—it's buried beneath it.

Isn't that where roots live?

Roots exist below the surface—hidden, out of sight. Because they are not easily visible, we tend to overlook them. Dysfunctional roots operate in the same way—they remain beneath the surface, subtly influencing our thoughts, emotions, and behaviors, making them difficult to recognize.

But here's the truth: If you're bold enough to dig deep, you will find the root of your issue. And if you are courageous enough to dig even deeper, you will discover its true source—an emotional wound that never fully healed.

Because emotional wounds are painful, we instinctively avoid letting anyone touch them. And too often, "anyone" includes our heavenly Father. But without God's supernatural healing, these wounds will keep us bound in cycles of self-destruction. We will continue bouncing from job to job, living paycheck to paycheck, dodging debt collectors, and moving from one dysfunctional relationship to another.

You can stop the cycle. You can put an end to self-sabotage.

Make a decision today: Start digging. Keep digging until you identify the root of your struggle and where it originated. Then surrender it to the Lord. Let Him touch the deepest wounds, the ones you've tried to ignore, and bring complete healing.

> LET HIM TOUCH THE DEEPEST WOUNDS, THE ONES YOU'VE TRIED TO IGNORE, AND BRING COMPLETE HEALING.

When you do, your perception will change. You will see clearly. You will discern what is good and what is harmful. You will avoid the pitfalls that once sabotaged your life.

BIRDS OF A FEATHER AND DYSFUNCTIONAL RELATIONSHIPS

There's an old adage that says, "Birds of a feather flock together." This statement rings especially true in the realm of dysfunctional relationships.

Dysfunctional people often have an unseen magnet within them—one that draws other dysfunctional people into their lives. It's almost as if they emit a silent signal that only those with similar dysfunctions can recognize.

This pattern is evident in common relationship dynamics, such as...

- An insecure man often attracts a controlling woman.
- A woman who feels worthless tends to be drawn to a man who is abusive.

Dysfunction recognizes dysfunction. And until healing takes place, the cycle continues.

As a pastor, I have counseled many women who have suffered verbal, physical, or emotional abuse. More often than not, they are passive, struggling to stand up for themselves. And they repeatedly find themselves drawn to men who are abusive and excessively controlling.

The question is, "Why are they attracted to this type of man, and why do they tend to stay in abusive relationships?" Is it possible that the abuse and control feed something deep within them?

Please allow me to explain. Every act of abuse wounds the person being mistreated. Each slap, each angry outburst, and every demeaning word inflicts both physical and emotional damage. But in a twisted way, it also validates something within them.

Even though they are devastated by the mistreatment, something inside them—whether insecurity, self-hatred, or unresolved trauma—feeds on the abuse. This is why many women struggle to leave relationships that bring them pain. As destructive as it is, something about it feels familiar. The abuse reinforces a preexisting sense of low self-worth and self-loathing.

Likewise, some men are repeatedly drawn to controlling women. Even though they dislike being controlled, they submit to it because yielding feels easier than confronting their own insecurities. A controlling partner exposes their lack of confidence and self-worth, validating a deficiency that already exists within them.

THE PRINCIPLE OF A MAGNET

Dysfunction attracts dysfunction, much like a magnetic field. For instance, those with unresolved rejection issues tend to gravitate toward people who will ultimately reject, abandon, or betray them. Subconsciously, they seek out individuals who will affirm and validate the rejection they already feel deep inside.

If, for some reason, someone fails to validate their rejection, they instinctively provoke rejection themselves. They may push the person away, act in a manner that invites abandonment, or misinterpret innocent actions as intentional rejection. Eventually, the person withdraws, leaving them abandoned once again. At that moment, they declare, "You see, they rejected me just like everybody else does."

We unconsciously set ourselves up to confirm our dysfunction—whether it's rejection, betrayal, abandonment, fear, or insecurity. It's the principle of a magnet: If our wounds remain unhealed, we will not only attract but also be drawn to those who will validate them. Why? Because dysfunction's survival depends on validation!

When dysfunction is validated, it secures a place of prominence in your life. The more it is reinforced, the stronger its grip becomes. Soon, it begins to dictate your emotions, shape your thoughts, influence your attitudes, and control your behaviors. You become a captive, no longer free.

THE PARASITE AND THE HOST

Dysfunctional behavior can be compared to the relationship between a parasite and its host. Just as a parasite relies on a host for survival, dysfunction needs something to feed on. If dysfunction is deprived of a host—something to cling to—it will eventually die. It cannot exist on its own.

Consider these interesting facts about parasites:

- Parasites benefit from a prolonged close association with the hosts, which are harmed by them.
- Parasites use many strategies for getting from one host to another.
- Parasites feed on other parasites.
- Parasites evolve in response to the defense mechanisms of their hosts.
- Parasites reduce host fitness.
- Parasites increase their fitness by exploiting hosts.[1]

This is why dysfunctional relationships are so difficult to break: because dysfunction is parasitical in nature, requiring something to feed on. When separation is suggested, it is often met with intense resistance.

Even if individuals agree to separate, it is usually only for a brief time. Sadly, the magnet principle prevails, and before long they are back to talking and texting. In no time, "the dysfunctional duo" is reunited, feeding off one another, despite the constant misunderstandings, manipulative behaviors, arguments, and, in some cases, even abuse. The parasitic relationship continues.

In situations like this, attraction or feelings of love are not enough to justify staying. If healing is the goal, separation is necessary until the "parasite" has been deprived of the "food" it thrives on. When it has nothing to feed on, it will die.

> YES, IT IS POSSIBLE TO HAVE RELATIONSHIPS FREE FROM CONTROL, MANIPULATION, ANGER, INSECURITY, GUILT TRIPS, THREATS, INTIMIDATION, FEAR, AND ABUSE. THE EMOTIONAL ROLLER COASTER CAN STOP.

The good news? Relationships don't have to be dysfunctional. They can be positive and "parasite-free"—healthy, thriving, and built on mutual respect.

Yes, it is possible to have relationships free from control, manipulation, anger, insecurity, guilt trips, threats, intimidation, fear, and abuse. The emotional roller coaster can stop.

Healing is possible. While no relationship is perfect, you can experience a relationship that is both healthy and secure.

Burgers or Sushi?

Hunger determines both what you crave and where you go to satisfy it. My wife and I love sushi, and when that craving hits, guess what we do? We jump in the car and head straight to our favorite sushi restaurant. Even though we enjoy a good burger from time to time, when we're hungry for sushi, nothing else will do.

On the way, our minds are already on our favorite dishes. We can almost taste the sushi before we even get there!

Hunger dictates what we are drawn to and the course we take in life. If there's a hunger inside of us for validation in our dysfunction, we will naturally follow the road to nowhere. That road is filled with hurt and disaster—a place where parasitic dysfunction flourishes, trapping us in an unending cycle.

To break free from the cycle of parasitic dysfunction, the decision is yours—and yours alone. You must choose to starve your dysfunction by cutting off every possible host, depriving it of its source of nourishment.

This means that if your dysfunction thrives in negative, abusive relationships, you must separate from those environments and begin surrounding yourself with individuals who uplift and encourage you. Fill yourself with God's Word and discover your true identity in Christ. Starve your dysfunction.

Keepin' It Real

I've had relationships at various times in my life that were driven by an unhealthy need.

When I first started out in ministry years ago, I still

carried pockets of insecurity that had not been dealt with. I recognized this because, at times, I felt uncomfortable—maybe even threatened—when I was around others who were thriving in areas where I was not.

Perhaps their preaching gift was more developed, or they were walking through open doors of opportunity that had not yet opened for me. I was genuinely happy for their success, but at the same time, I felt threatened by it! Until I allowed healing to take place, I surrounded myself with people who didn't challenge me—which only limited how far I could go in life.

As I became whole, I intentionally surrounded myself with people who were further along than I was. Soon, I discovered that by doing this, I was growing and stepping into things I had never thought possible. The enemy had a devious plan to use my insecurities to stunt my growth and development, but his plan was defeated when I allowed God to heal this issue.

I came to realize that true success in life and ministry has very little to do with large crowds, abundant resources, or great notoriety. It has everything to do with being a healthy, secure leader—one who can lead others into the same wholeness they have personally experienced.

As I said earlier, you must deprive the dysfunction of its host. Healing begins when you recognize the signs. If you're in a relationship that continuously pulls you into a self-destructive cycle, it's time to step away.

If the troubled area is your marriage, begin setting healthy boundaries. If insecurities or other struggles keep resurfacing, stop feeding the dysfunction. Deprive it of its host. Instead, fill your life with God's Word and allow the Truth to draw you closer to Jesus—your Healer.

MAGNETISM OR MALFUNCTION?

We talked about magnets before. What happens when magnets are near each other? I'm not a scientist, nor do I claim to fully understand the physics behind it. But one thing I do know: When opposite charges are near each other, they attract. Have you ever heard the old adage "opposites attract"?

That principle may work in a science experiment, but when it comes to dysfunctional relationships, it often leads to disaster. For example, someone who's controlling will naturally attract someone who has an emotional need to be controlled. An overachiever will be drawn to someone who avoids responsibility. An overly emotional person will attract someone emotionally shut down. Someone who is insecure will attract a domineering personality. In these types of relationships, dysfunction fuels dysfunction.

This may be difficult to grasp, but when you become emotionally healthy, dysfunction will no longer be drawn to you. Instead of attracting it, you'll begin to repel it.

Why? Because those who thrive on dysfunction will quickly realize you're no longer a willing participant in their cycle. And parasites don't stick around where they can't feed. Their hunger remains, but your kitchen is closed!

When you are healed, you won't need to announce it to those with whom you've been in a dysfunctional relationship. They will either pursue healing along with you, or they will take their dysfunction elsewhere.

It's time for your perception to be healed. Do you want to continue seeing "men as trees, walking," or do you want to see with clarity? If you're ready to see clearly, then it's time to stop viewing your present through the filter of past injuries.

Just as the blind man was healed from the injury that damaged his sight, he began to see everything for what it truly was—men as men, good as good, bad as bad, blessing as blessing, and dysfunction as dysfunction. What overwhelming joy he must have felt to finally see with clarity!

Now imagine the joy that awaits you as your perceptions are healed. As you release the lens of past wounds, you will begin to see with sharpness, accuracy, and discernment. Your entire decision-making process will transform. You will walk in wisdom, make healthy choices, and build strong, fulfilling relationships. No longer will false perceptions sabotage your life—you will be seeing with new eyes!

Let the Healing Begin

My prayer is that you will have the courage and strength to actively pursue your healing. Healing won't chase you down—it requires you to go after it. It won't happen just because you're miserable, depressed, or hurt. Healing comes to those who refuse to stay bound by their pain and who relentlessly pursue freedom.

"Want to" must meet "have to." It's not enough to

simply want healing. You must declare, "I have to have it, and I won't stop until I get it!"

I encourage you to open your heart and allow the Lord to uncover the roots of your pain. Are you willing to do whatever it takes to be healed, even if it hurts?

If you are willing to face the pain, you will step into the abundant life that awaits you!

Prayer

In Jesus' name, I break the power of sabotage over my life. As I walk in healing, I will no longer attract unhealthy things and people. I don't just want healing; I am determined not to stop until I get it! I won't relent. I won't stop. I will not quit. Healing and wholeness are mine. Amen.

Chapter 15

RELIEF OR CURE?

DO YOU EVER feel as though you're merely surviving, just trying to make it through one more day? Dysfunction has a way of locking us into survival mode. I don't believe the Lord wants anyone to live that way. He doesn't want us to settle for short-term relief when He offers lasting freedom. He wants so much more than temporary survival—He desires for us to live abundantly, free from dysfunction, filled with joy, walking in wholeness.

Mark 10 tells the familiar account of a blind man named Bartimaeus. Many focus on the dramatic moment of his healing but miss the deeper impact of what truly happened in this man's life.

> And when he heard that it was Jesus of Nazareth, he began to cry out and say, "Jesus, Son of David, have mercy on me!" Then many warned him to be quiet; but he cried out all the more, "Son of David, have mercy on me!"
>
> —MARK 10:47–48

Blind Bartimaeus sat along the roadside, begging for his survival. His blindness left him with no way to work or provide for himself, forcing him into a life of poverty and dependence. Without the charity of others, he would have starved to death.

Day after day, the cycle repeated. He reached out his hand, pleading for food or pocket change. Some days he received more than others, but never enough. At the end of the day, he would eat just enough to quiet the hunger pangs before lying down somewhere on the street to sleep. And when morning came, the cycle began again.

Each new day was the same. Awakened by hunger, he knew that if he didn't beg, he wouldn't eat. So he begged. And begged. And begged—just to find relief. But relief was always temporary.

Bartimaeus wasn't living. He was surviving. Every day was about making it through one more day. Sitting by the roadside, cloaked in darkness, he waited—hoping someone might show him kindness, offer him a few coins, or give him just enough to sustain him.

THE CRY FOR MERCY

When Jesus left Jericho, a great multitude followed Him. As the crowd moved closer, Bartimaeus heard that Jesus was headed his way.

From his reaction, it was clear he knew something about Jesus' reputation. Perhaps his heart leaped with expectation as he contemplated receiving a long-awaited miracle. Desperate to be healed, he seized the moment and cried out, "Jesus, Son of David, have mercy on me!"

His need was great, and he refused to be ignored. He wasn't begging for bread or spare change—he was pleading for a miracle.

> And when he heard that it was Jesus of Nazareth, he began to cry out and say, "Jesus, Son of David, have mercy on me!"
>
> —Mark 10:47

The cries of Bartimaeus stirred opposition. Some in the crowd rebuked him, sternly ordering him to be quiet. But Bartimaeus would not be silenced. Determined to reach Jesus, he cried out even louder, "Son of David, have mercy on me!" (Mark 10:48).

His desperate cry stopped Jesus in His tracks. Moved with compassion, Jesus commanded the crowd to bring him near.

> Then they called the blind man, saying to him, "Be of good cheer. Rise, He is calling you." And throwing aside his garment, he rose and came to Jesus.
>
> —Mark 10:49–50

This was his moment. Nothing could keep him from the Master now! As soon as Jesus called for him, Bartimaeus threw aside his garment and rose to go. At first glance, this act may seem insignificant, but it was a powerful declaration of faith.

Some scholars suggest that blind individuals were identified by a special type of garment. It signified their condition, making it easier for the community to recognize their need and offer help. For Bartimaeus, this cloak was more than clothing—it symbolized his identity as a blind beggar.

Casting it aside was a bold step. Though he was still blind, he released his dependence on what had once

Relief or Cure?

sustained him, stepping forward in faith. He no longer clung to the identity of a blind man. This was his moment to receive a new name, a new future. No longer "blind" Bartimaeus, the beggar—but "healed" Bartimaeus, the man who once was blind but now could see!

Perhaps he reached his hands out before him, moving slowly in the direction of Jesus' voice. We don't know how long it took him to get there, but when he finally arrived, Jesus asked him, "What do you want Me to do for you?"

Full of faith and expectation, Bartimaeus replied without hesitation, "Rabboni, that I may receive my sight."

> So Jesus answered and said to him, "What do you want Me to do for you?" The blind man said to Him, "Rabboni, that I may receive my sight." Then Jesus said to him, "Go your way; your faith has made you well." And immediately he received his sight and followed Jesus on the road.
> —MARK 10:51–52

SEEING THROUGH NEW EYES

Although Bartimaeus's blindness was evident, Jesus did not assume his request. Instead, He asked, "What do you want Me to do for you?"

It is important to remember that God always knows what we need—even better than we do. Yet He still asks, "What do you want Me to do for you?"

Bartimaeus's response reveals a powerful truth. Even though he had lived in poverty, he did not ask for money or material provision. Financial support would have provided only temporary relief—helping him survive one more day. But he wanted more than survival. He recognized that his blindness was the root of his lack, so his request cut straight to the heart of the matter: "Lord, that I might receive my sight."

He wasn't asking for a quick fix—he was asking for complete restoration. He wanted a cure, not just relief. He was done with survival mode. He wanted more than another day of begging—he wanted to see with new eyes!

DOUBLE FAVOR

When Bartimaeus received his sight, he was no longer trapped in blindness and helplessness. The condition that once confined him was gone, and he stepped from darkness into light. With his sight restored, he was no longer dependent on the generosity of others—he could work, earn a living, and move forward in freedom. His days of begging were over!

When Jesus heard Bartimaeus's cry for mercy, He responded with double favor—Bartimaeus was no longer blind, and he was no longer a beggar. He was made whole.

> Then Jesus said to him, "Go your way; your faith has made you well." And immediately he received his sight and followed Jesus on the road.
> —MARK 10:52

Imagine what Bartimaeus must have felt as his eyes opened for the first time. The very first image he saw was the face of Jesus! Overwhelmed, he must have stood in awe—speechless—taking in the miracle that had just unfolded before him.

Relief or Cure?

In response to this life-changing moment, Bartimaeus's gratitude moved him to immediate action—he followed Jesus without hesitation. He didn't rush off to tell his family or friends. He had been set free, and his only desire was to follow the One who had restored him.

Everything was different! No longer the poor, blind beggar who once relied on others to guide him, Bartimaeus walked with confidence. He wasn't stumbling or falling. His steps were steady. His heart was full. His eyes were clear. Healed and whole, he fixed his gaze on Jesus and never looked back.

Before Bartimaeus was healed, he wore the garment of a blind beggar. What about you? What garment are you still wearing? The garment of past hurt? The garment of abuse? The garment of betrayal? The garment of rejection? The garment of abandonment? The garment of family iniquity? The garment of a victim?

> WHEN GIVEN THE OPPORTUNITY TO BRING YOUR PETITION BEFORE GOD, WILL YOU SETTLE FOR TEMPORARY RELIEF, OR WILL YOU PRESS IN FOR A PERMANENT CURE?

As Bartimaeus arose and moved toward Jesus, desperate for his miracle, he cast off his garment—he let go of what once defined him. Are you desperate enough to do the same? When those around you try to silence your cry for mercy, will you lift your voice even louder? Will you refuse to let embarrassment and shame hold you back?

When given the opportunity to bring your petition

before God, will you settle for temporary relief, or will you press in for a permanent cure?

RELIEF OR CURE?

Sadly, over the years, I have watched people come to church in their "Sunday best" with a "relief mentality" rather than seeking a permanent cure that would free them from their dysfunction and bring true healing to their lives.

Here are a few examples of a relief mentality:

- "Hopefully, the pastor will preach a message to pump me up so I can make it one more day..."
- "Hopefully, praise and worship will be good so I can forget about my problems for a little while..."
- "Hopefully, the service will help me get my mind off my troubles and make me feel like I can go on..."

If we're honest, we've all been guilty of making church about relief rather than a cure.

When people go to church with this mindset, they wake up Monday morning trapped in the same neverending cycle of survival mode. The words of relief they heard the day before fade into a distant memory, and soon, they crave another emotional pick-me-up. But they fail to realize that Jesus did not come to be a temporary relief—He came to be the solution! They don't have to just barely survive, trudging through life, slapping one

Band-Aid on after another. The cycle can end. Jesus came to give life—and life more abundantly!

The Power of the Word

God's Word is powerful and provides more than just relief. If you open your heart and surrender to Him, the Word will not only touch your emotions but transform your character. It will invade every part of your life and change you, bringing permanent solutions that make you whole—spirit, soul, and body.

Look at Bartimaeus. His begging only brought temporary relief, not a permanent solution. His problem wasn't a lack of alms; it was his blindness. His inability to see prohibited him from working, earning a living, and living in freedom. But Jesus went straight to the root of the issue. He didn't bring him relief—He brought him a cure.

> HEALING REQUIRES MORE THAN JUST RECOGNIZING THE NEED FOR CHANGE— IT DEMANDS ACTION.

Healing requires more than just recognizing the need for change—it demands action. Like Bartimaeus, you must be willing to cast off the old, cry out for mercy, and step into the healing Jesus offers. Your past does not define you, nor does your pain have to control you. Freedom is available, but the choice is yours. Will you embrace it?

PRAYER

Dear Jesus, I know You died for me. Your sacrifice was and is complete. You did not suffer just so I would know relief. You bled and died so that I can have the cure. Help me to never settle for relief. I am going after the cure! In Your name, amen.

Chapter 16

GET TO THE ROOT

IN THE NATURAL world, a tree's health and strength are at risk if there's a problem at the root. You can't get to the root of the problem without digging through some dirt.

In the same way, we must dig through the dirt of our dysfunction to expose the root cause of why we do what we do. But, too often, we focus only on the symptoms we can see above the surface and search for quick fixes to eliminate them. Somehow, we convince ourselves that if the symptoms disappear, everything will be okay. But unless we dig deep and uncover the true cause, we'll never achieve lasting wholeness.

> Even now the axe is laid to the root of the trees.
> Every tree therefore that does not bear good fruit
> is cut down and thrown into the fire.
> —MATTHEW 3:10, ESV

In the story of blind Bartimaeus, there was one obvious symptom—poverty. If a generous donor had given him enough wealth to live comfortably for the rest

HEALING HURTS

of his life, the symptom of poverty would have vanished. But he still would have remained blind, unable to fully function in his life. Eliminating one symptom would have made him better—but not whole.

When Bartimaeus allowed Jesus to get to the root of his problem, everything changed. Not only was his blindness healed, but his entire life was transformed. His days of begging were over. His identity was restored. His future was rewritten.

> THE QUESTION IS NOT WHAT YOU DO—IT'S WHY YOU DO IT.

I challenge you today to dig deep. Find the root cause of your dysfunctional behaviors. The question is not what you do—it's why you do it. When you uncover the why, you've found the root. That's when true healing can begin—eliminating not just one symptom, but all of them!

DIG AND KEEP ON DIGGING

In Christianity, we have become professionals at identifying the "fruit" but have failed miserably at identifying the "root." We need to ask ourselves, "Why do we do what we do? Why do we act the way we act? Why does money seem to fall through invisible holes in our pockets? Why do our relationships keep falling apart? Why can't we hold a steady job? What happened to bring us to this place?"

Throughout my years in ministry, I have encountered many different types of people within the church. Each one has a story. Each one has struggles. Each one has a root cause behind their dysfunction. Let's look at four different types of people to illustrate how to get to the root of the problem and finally be made whole.

As you read these examples, my prayer is that you will gain insight into your own life and recognize how to receive a permanent solution to your struggles—not just temporary relief.

1. THE LONELY ONE

The lonely person is lonely wherever they are—in a crowd, at the office, at a family reunion, or sitting at home alone. No matter where they go, they feel isolated and disconnected. In fact, if it were possible, their picture would appear next to the word "lonely" in the dictionary!

An individual like this can be found in the most unexpected places. They might be married with a large family, yet they are still lonely. They could have more friends and acquaintances than they know what to do with, yet loneliness still lingers.

Lonely people find temporary relief from their loneliness by numbing the root cause in different ways. Most often, they try to drown out the loneliness by staying busy—always moving, always doing. Busy, busy, busy... that's how they strive to live each day. Idle time is intimidating, so they fill their schedules with an endless list of activities. They even insert themselves into situations where they're neither needed nor wanted, just to feel connected. But at the end of the day, their hectic, exhausting schedule leaves them feeling just as empty—and still lonely.

No matter how many friends they have, no matter how many people love them, no matter how many lunch invitations they accept each week, they still go to bed at night feeling alone. Why? Because they have settled for the pocket change of temporary relief rather than receiving the permanent solution. They have filled their life with distractions, yet the loneliness remains.

Many of the branded pain relievers at your local pharmacy promise powerful relief. But no matter how good the product is, if you have a broken leg, pain relief won't heal it. The medication may dull the pain for a time, but once it wears off, the problem is still there. The same is true for loneliness. It's not relief that we need—it's healing. And that permanent healing is found only in Jesus Christ.

If you struggle with loneliness, let's not just deal with the symptoms. Let's go deeper and ask the real question: Why are you lonely? Did something traumatic happen in your life that damaged your ability to bond? Were you abandoned as a child by a parent, leaving you afraid to connect with others, fearing they will also leave? Were you neglected or abused, causing you to withdraw from emotional attachment? Were you betrayed by someone you trusted, leaving you trapped inside an impenetrable wall of self-protection?

What is the root of your loneliness?

2. The Miserable and Depressed One

Depression is a growing problem worldwide. Each year I meet more and more individuals who have either suffered from depression themselves or walked alongside a

Get to the Root

loved one battling it. It affects people of all ages, races, and economic levels.

I recognize that depression can stem from multiple sources. At times, it is biological, caused by chemical imbalances or genetic disorders. Other times, it is rooted in trauma or tragedy—grief over the death of a loved one, a failed marriage, a financial crisis, victimization, abandonment, rejection, betrayal, loss of employment, physical illness—the list goes on. Regardless of the cause, depression is debilitating and miserable.

Medical professionals often try to manage depression by prescribing anti-depressants. These medications mask the symptoms, providing temporary relief. But what happens when the medication is stopped? In most cases, the depression remains.

Have you ever seen television commercials for prescription products, especially anti-depressants? They highlight "life-changing results" but quickly follow up with disclaimers like "Common side effects include insomnia, nausea, anxiety, dry mouth, headaches, loss of appetite, suicidal tendencies..." and much, much more! The side effects often sound worse than the problem itself. Temporary relief at best...certainly not a cure!

Because depression is so miserable, those who suffer from it tend to gravitate toward addictive behaviors. When we think about addiction, our minds often go straight to substances like illicit drugs or alcohol. But addiction isn't limited to substances. It can be anything used to escape from misery.

People who are depressed tend to self-medicate to numb their pain and artificially lift their spirits. Some turn to drugs or alcohol, but others turn to shopping.

Yes, spending money can be an addiction! Studies have been done on compulsive shoppers and hoarders, whose homes are filled with mountains of unnecessary "stuff," all collected in an attempt to soothe an inner void.

The list of addictions is endless: pornography, gambling, eating disorders, excessive exercising, dieting, oversleeping, gaming, social media, sexual dependencies, smoking, prescription drugs, workaholism, binge-watching, toxic relationships, co-dependency, self-harm—the list goes on. Anything you feel compelled to do, even when you don't want to, is an addiction. Any habit used to escape reality and numb emotional pain is a form of addiction.

Regardless of the addiction, it is nothing more than a way to escape pain temporarily. But temporary relief always demands another "fix." It never leads to healing—only a cycle of emptiness, self-destruction, and misery. At the end of the day, they are still depressed and miserable.

Look at Hollywood celebrities or famous musicians. They appear to have it all—success, fame, and millions of dollars. Yet many of them tragically die premature deaths, lost in addiction, loneliness, and despair. The drugs, the partying, the extravagant lifestyles might have provided relief for a time, but the root of their pain was never healed. Their success and fortune were not enough. They were left searching for more, only to find an emptiness they could never fill.

Depression doesn't discriminate. It affects people from all walks of life—including Christians. Sadly, I've even known successful pastors of large churches who struggled with such intense depression that they took

Get to the Root

their own lives. How could this happen? They knew Jesus. They knew His Word. Yet depression still overtook them.

As a PK (pastor's kid), I watched my father battle depression firsthand. He was a gifted man of God who loved the Lord with all his heart. He planted a church that quickly became the largest in our community. We had a thriving Christian school. People traveled long distances to attend our services. Miracles happened weekly. Yet despite all the outward success, depression was still there.

Ultimately, my father's unresolved depression led to a struggle with sin, unraveling our lives completely.

But in the midst of the chaos, my father made the brave decision to seek help. He checked himself into an inpatient Christian counseling center, where psychological testing revealed something shocking—he had suffered from major depression since early childhood.

He was stunned. Even more shocking was the revelation that depression is often "anger turned inward." He had no idea he was even angry! After all, he was the life of the party. His laughter could be heard over any crowd. Anger? What could he possibly be angry about?

But as he kept digging through the dirt of his past, the truth surfaced. Yes, he was angry—very angry. Things had happened in his childhood that deeply wounded him. But as a child, he didn't know how to process that anger, so he buried it. Out of sight, out of mind...right? Wrong.

According to an article on Harvard Business School's website, the subconscious mind controls 95 percent of your life. Today's science estimates that the vast majority of our decisions, actions, emotions, and behaviors are driven by subconscious programming.[1]

As children, we often don't have the tools to properly process anger. So, we shove it deep into our subconscious minds, ignoring and burying it. We assume if we don't think about it, it no longer exists. But what we've buried is still alive, working behind the scenes, wreaking havoc in our lives—without our permission. Even if we're not consciously aware of it, it's still controlling our attitudes, behaviors, and decisions. This is why so many people find themselves trapped in destructive cycles, wondering why they can't break free.

For my father, digging through the dirt of his childhood was painful. Nobody enjoys confronting the wounds of their past. But as he continued to open his heart, allowing the Lord to bring healing, he finally experienced freedom. All the internalized anger was released in a healthy way.

> WHAT WE'VE BURIED IS STILL ALIVE, WORKING BEHIND THE SCENES, WREAKING HAVOC IN OUR LIVES—WITHOUT OUR PERMISSION.

He no longer suffers from depression. The addiction is gone. For the first time, he knows what it is to experience true joy and fulfillment.

3. The Insecure One

Based on years of ministry experience, I have found that insecurity is one of the most prevalent struggles among believers. While it is true that insecure people lack an understanding of who they are in Christ, that lack of understanding comes from somewhere. Before we get to the root, let's examine some of the behaviors—both overt and subtle—that insecurity produces.

Insecure people often struggle with self-hatred and rejection, but at the same time, they seek external validation to give them a sense of well-being. They crave approval and acceptance because their sense of identity, worth, and value is entirely dependent on how others perceive them. This deep-seated need drives them to seek validation from people, mistakenly believing that if others affirm them, they will finally feel loved, needed, and important.

However, this desperate pursuit of validation is a setup for disappointment. Most often, when an insecure person helps someone, their heart is well-intentioned, but their motive is unhealthy.

Let me explain. Insecure people are good people, but without realizing it, they often have ulterior motives behind their "good deeds." They attach strings to their actions, expecting something in return—praise, acceptance, approval, recognition. To them, that equals love! They will do almost anything to receive it, including resorting to subtle manipulation and control.

Unfortunately, no amount of human affirmation will ever satisfy them. No matter how many pats on the back they receive, it's never enough to make them feel truly secure. This is why insecure people are often easily offended and tend to go from one relationship to another, constantly searching for fulfillment that always seems just out of reach.

Some insecure people attempt to fill the void with success. They believe their worth is measured by the car they drive, the house they live in, the money in their bank account, the designer labels they wear, or the accomplishments they achieve. But no matter how much they acquire, it never silences the nagging voice of insecurity. The real issue is much deeper. What is it inside them that drives them to seek success as their source of worth?

Insecurity is often masked by an outward display of pride and arrogance. In fact, I believe the true definition of pride is insecurity. The most prideful people are often the most insecure. They brag about their successes, name-drop the influential people they know, and flaunt their material possessions—but beneath it all, they are desperately trying to convince both themselves and others that they matter. Deep down, they feel inadequate and empty.

Insecure people tend to become professional mask wearers. They smile on the outside, but inside, they are miserable. They may project confidence, but in reality, they are unhappy with who they think they are.

If you struggle with insecurity, I challenge you to dig deep and ask, "What is the root cause?" In my experience, insecurity is almost always traced back to unmet needs in childhood.

One of the most fundamental needs of a child is to feel protected by their parents. If a parent is absent—whether by choice, illness, work, addiction, imprisonment, or death—the result is the same. The child is left without the sense of security they so desperately need. This often leads to feelings of abandonment, loneliness, rejection, fear, unworthiness, and self-doubt.

The more unmet needs a person experiences in childhood, the more deeply rooted their insecurity becomes. And I can personally testify to this truth.

Even though my parents loved me with everything in them, they failed to meet my need for security. When I was twelve, their marriage fell apart. They were drowning in their own pain and couldn't help me navigate mine. I became a very insecure young man, acting out with unhealthy behaviors.

But I am incredibly grateful that my parents pursued their healing and freedom. Eventually, their healing led to my own, and I was able to step into a life of true security in Christ.

4. THE FEARFUL ONE

Fearful people live in torment. They are anxious about everything—their past, their present, their future, their finances, their job, what others think of them, and even things that might never happen. They fear rejection, betrayal, abandonment, failure, success, disapproval, the unknown, commitment, being hurt, not being good enough, expectations, responsibility, and being taken advantage of.

Fearful people are also controlling people. They feverishly try to control situations to protect themselves and create a sense of safety. They even try to control others—sometimes with good intentions—believing they are "helping," even when their help is unrequested and unappreciated.

Because fearful people struggle to trust, they feel the need to be in charge of everything. But when life inevitably spins out of control, their world is rocked, and their security is shaken. In a panic, they do whatever it takes to regain control. They lie, cover up, hide, deceive, manipulate, blame, and engage in a whole host of self-defeating behaviors—all in a desperate attempt to restore their illusion of safety.

Fearful people struggle with integrity because they are afraid of the truth and the consequences it may bring. When Adam and Eve sinned in the garden, their first response was to run away and hide. They went to great lengths to cover their nakedness with fig leaves, expecting God not to notice. But He did.

When the Lord inquired about their actions, they had a rational, justified excuse.

"We had to cover up because we were naked," they said.

God responded, "Who told you that you were naked?"

Immediately, Adam shifted the blame. "Lord, this woman you gave me..." In other words, "It's Eve's fault—and actually, God, it's Your fault for giving her to me."

Then God turned to Eve and asked, "What have you done?"

She quickly responded, "The serpent deceived me, and I ate." Translation: "It's not my fault. The devil made me do it" (paraphrased from Genesis 3:10–13).

Neither Adam nor Eve had the integrity to take responsibility. Why? Fear kept them from owning their actions, so they shifted blame instead of repenting.

Even though fearful people crave control, the truth is, they are the ones who are controlled—controlled by fear itself. It compels them to cover up, lie, and deceive, even when they don't realize they're doing it.

You might be thinking, "I don't do that." But let me ask you: How many times have you said, "That didn't hurt me," when it really did? How many times have you insisted, "I don't need help," when you were struggling? How many times have you declared, "I'm fine," when you knew deep down you weren't?

Fearful people lie not only with their words but also with their nonverbal expressions. They wear masks, pasting on false smiles. They say the right things, look put-together on the outside, and pretend everything is fine—even when their world is crumbling. They fear admitting their struggles, showing weakness, or appearing vulnerable.

At its core, fear is a lack of trust in God. Fearful people build walls around their hearts, convinced those walls will protect them. But those walls keep God out too. And unless they choose to surrender, to lay down their need for control, not even God will force His way in.

Do you struggle with fear? If so, what is at the root?

It's time to close that door and uproot the stronghold of fear. It's time to allow the love of God to have its perfect work in you.

> There is no fear in love, but perfect love casts out fear.
> —1 John 4:18, mev

Dig Until You're Free

Too often, we settle for treating symptoms instead of addressing the root of our dysfunction. We convince ourselves that if we can just fix what's visible—our loneliness, depression, insecurity, or fear—then everything will be fine. But deep down, we know better. The real problem isn't what's happening on the surface; it's what's buried beneath.

Like a tree with unhealthy roots, our struggles stem from something deeper—something that has taken hold and shaped the way we see ourselves and the world around us. Until we are willing to dig through the dirt, expose what's hidden, and let God uproot the source, we will continue to repeat the same cycles.

You don't have to live in survival mode. You don't have to keep masking the pain. Whether your struggle is loneliness, misery, insecurity, or fear, God wants to bring healing—not just relief. He wants to go beyond the surface and set you free at the root. But it's up to you. You must choose to dig, to face what's been buried, and to surrender it to Him.

Wholeness is possible. Freedom is possible. Healing is yours for the taking. Are you ready to dig?

Prayer

Dear heavenly Father, today I claim victory over loneliness, depression, insecurity, and fear. I thank You, Holy Spirit, for helping me identify these strongholds, but I also pray that You help me identify the root. I'm willing to dig. I'm willing to get dirty and messy at all costs. I will go after the root. I will find wholeness. In Jesus' name, amen.

Chapter 17

THE SOLUTION

FREQUENTLY, IN MY travels, pastors, leaders, and businesspeople ask about our church in Orlando. One of the things I am most thankful for is the high percentage of volunteers who actively serve each week. Almost 80 percent of our church family is involved in some capacity—whether it's ushering, kids' ministry, youth ministry, the connection team, or connect groups. Over the years, this has amazed many leaders, and they often ask, "What's your secret?" My answer is always the same: When people begin to experience wholeness, they cannot wait to serve! A person's "want to" and their ability "to do" are directly tied to their health. When people get healed, they get busy!

As a pastor, it is my job to help those who desire healing discover the underlying issues preventing them from being whole. This requires an investment of time and patience. It's not as simple as saying, "Just do this, and all will be well." Real healing demands an internal search, a discovery of the root.

Sadly, I've had people come to me with sincere hearts, saying, "Pastor, I've been in church after church, but I'm still bound by this issue. I'm so frustrated because people keep telling me I need to be free, but nobody tells me how. I desperately want to be free, but I have no idea how to do it."

No auto mechanic screams at a broken-down car, commanding it to start. That won't fix the problem. He gets out his tools, gets his hands dirty, and repairs what's wrong. Likewise, no doctor looks at a broken bone that requires surgery and simply declares, "Be fixed! Bones, be unbroken!" They perform surgery, correct the issue, and begin the healing process.

What good would it do if, as a pastor, I simply barked out orders to someone whose life is governed by fear and insecurity?

- "Go be a great mom or dad!"
- "Go be successful in business!"
- "Go find happiness and fulfillment!"

For the person struggling with fear, those commands don't bring freedom. Instead, they feel the weight of inadequacy. "I can't do those things! I want to, but I feel like a failure. I lack confidence. I need help. I need to be healed."

My mission as a pastor and spiritual leader is not to give orders and mandates but to help bring God's healing anointing to those laid up in their sickbeds—whether physically, emotionally, or spiritually. The Holy Spirit is the One who reveals the *how*. And when that happens, those who were once bound by dysfunction will rise in healing and wholeness. They will be equipped to serve, empowered to succeed in their purpose, and ready to receive their marching orders.

The Solution

DEAL WITH THE ROOT

How do you find the solution? First, you need to stop investing all your energy into alleviating the symptoms. The symptoms are "what" you do because of a hidden issue. Instead, you need to do whatever it takes to uncover that hidden issue. This means you must start digging and keep digging until you reach the root—because the root is the *why* behind the *what*.

Think of it this way. Imagine someone experiencing an abnormal, unquenchable thirst. No matter how much water they drink, their thirst remains. Drinking excessive amounts of water is *what* they do—it's their symptom. But no matter how much they drink, the thirst won't go away. Eventually, they become desperate enough to dig deeper, and after seeking medical help, they discover the *why*. They have diabetes or some other underlying condition. Until that issue is exposed, it cannot be treated, and the symptoms will persist.

In my years of ministry, I've seen this pattern repeatedly. People spend hours talking about the *what*, expecting a simple solution to bring immediate relief. The *what* is often shocking, disturbing, and harmful, but the real question that must be answered is "Why?" Why do they keep doing what they do?

As a pastor, I believe I have a responsibility to help people uncover their *why*. If we fail to address the root, their symptoms will remain.

A common example is alcohol addiction. An alcoholic drinks too much. That's *what* they do. To stop the behavior, they might establish external controls—avoiding bars, staying away from certain people, or having an accountability partner. While these safeguards are useful, they don't address the deeper issue. What's driving their need to drink? What pain are they trying to numb? When external controls are removed, the urge to drink resurfaces, and the cycle begins again.

The real issue is always internal. I've walked with people who have struggled for years until they finally uncovered their hidden issue—the *why* behind their addiction. And when they surrendered it to the Holy Spirit, I watched them experience true freedom. The desire to drink completely vanished—not because of external controls, but because they were healed from the inside out.

We have to stop looking in the wrong places. The symptoms are not the real problem. The key is searching below the surface. Dig deep. Look within. When you do, you will get to the root of the issue—and that's when you will finally experience true healing through Jesus Christ.

It's time to stop searching in the wrong places. It's time to go to the root!

PERCEPTION PROBLEMS

In life, no one escapes injury. We live in a fallen world, surrounded by imperfect people who, knowingly or unknowingly, hurt us. We all suffer traumatic experiences. If we allow our wounds to go untreated, they will become infected, distorting our perceptions. "The heart

> IT'S TIME TO STOP SEARCHING IN THE WRONG PLACES. IT'S TIME TO GO TO THE ROOT!

The Solution

is deceitful above all things, and desperately wicked; who can know it?" (Jer. 17:9). When we see through the lens of past hurts, dysfunctions such as fear, insecurity, depression, rejection, abandonment, shame, and anger take root. Even if the injury occurred in childhood, it will continue to shape our lives.

Your healing is not just for you—it's for others. Your spouse, your children, your friends, your coworkers, your neighbors, your church family. God has called you to be a light in this dark world (Matt. 5:14–16) and to serve those around you (Gal. 5:13). But you cannot fully walk in this calling unless you are healed. We see this clearly illustrated in the account of Peter's mother-in-law, who was unable to serve because she was sick with a fever.

> Now when Jesus had come into Peter's house, He saw his wife's mother lying sick with a fever. So He touched her hand, and the fever left her. And she arose and served them.
> —MATTHEW 8:14–15

When Jesus entered Peter's house, He saw Peter's mother-in-law lying in bed, feverish and unable to function. With one touch, He healed her, and the fever left immediately.

What was the first thing she did after being healed? She got up and served those in the house! Her purpose was to serve. But before Jesus touched her, she couldn't function in that purpose. Once she was healed, she was released into it.

Over the years, I've watched many people burning with the "fever" of dysfunction—frustrated because, no matter how hard they tried, they couldn't fully walk in their purpose. They didn't realize they needed healing before they could step into their callings.

God has given you a purpose. You are called to serve! But first you must seek healing. As healing comes, you will be released into your purpose. You will be transformed and set free from every "fever" of dysfunction. You will be healed to serve, function wholly, and fulfill your destiny.

If It Happened Today

The outcome of Peter's mother-in-law's story might have been drastically different if it had been handled by a modern-day spiritual leader. Too often, pastors and those in spiritual authority are more interested in people's gifts than in their wholeness. Instead of asking, "What can I give them?" the mentality has become "What can they give me?" This mindset has created a culture where obvious dysfunction and even blatant sin are ignored simply because someone has an incredible skill set. Within this culture, people are told just to "push through" and serve—no matter what.

> You will be healed to serve, function wholly, and fulfill your destiny.

Being respectful, the individual drags themselves out of bed, attempting to "push through" and serve those in the house, not realizing that they are infecting everyone they serve. The result is always the same: disaster! Why?

The Solution

Because fever spreads. And when someone has a fever, that is when they are the most contagious.

From the moment Jesus entered Peter's house, He did not ignore the fever of Peter's mother-in-law. "Now when Jesus had come into Peter's house, He saw his wife's mother lying sick with a fever. So He touched her hand, and the fever left her. And she arose and served them" (Matt. 8:14–15). Notice He didn't tell her to "push through" and start serving despite her condition. He didn't rebuke her for failing to fulfill her calling. Instead, He rebuked the very thing that was keeping her from it! Jesus went right to the root, identifying the cause of her affliction. He rebuked the fever that was hindering her. And then—only then—she was able to rise and serve.

It's time for you to be liberated from your dysfunctions, insecurities, and fears. This is your moment to be set free! Allow Jesus to touch you and watch the "fever" of past hurts and wounds leave. It's time for you to serve. It's time for you to fulfill your calling and purpose. It's time for you to step into an abundant life!

PRAYER

Father, this is my day of freedom. I want to be healed from my past so I can be who You've called me to be. I'm tired of temporary relief— I'm ready for You to bring the solution. Where I have been bound, I declare that I am free. I receive liberty in every area of captivity. I will serve. I will fulfill my calling and purpose. I will face the pain and step into an abundant life! Amen.

Chapter 18

GETTING STARTED

As I mentioned previously, we are all a work in progress and will continue to be as long as we live on earth. Each of us has our own "stuff to deal with." While I have never been afflicted with leprosy like Naaman or been blind like Bartimaeus, I can relate to these examples because I have dealt with my own dysfunction. The dysfunctions I faced in my past crippled me and held me captive. My deliverance came only when I surrendered to the healing process, just as Naaman and Bartimaeus did.

The message of *Healing Hurts* is my story. The principles I have shared with you on the pages of this book chart the lessons learned in my journey to find wholeness.

Even though the process of healing hurts, it's the right kind of hurt—one that brings healing, deliverance, and freedom. As you go through this painful process, be encouraged. The hurt is not a forever kind of hurt. It's temporary. But the change you experience will be permanent and will bring you real joy.

> Jesus Christ is the same yesterday, today, and forever.
>
> —Hebrews 13:8

It is my desire that, as you have read each page of this book, your heart has been opened to a supernatural, life-changing experience with God. Scripture reminds us: "Jesus Christ is the same yesterday, today, and forever" (Heb. 13:8). He never changes, and He stands ready to touch and transform your life starting today. Only He can set you free and make you whole.

> Jesus Christ is the same yesterday, today, and forever.
> —Hebrews 13:8

Are you ready? Do you really want it? Do you want it, even if it hurts? His anointing destroys every yoke of bondage. His power is potent and overcomes every stronghold. He's waiting, with arms wide open, to heal every damaged emotion and to liberate you from all dysfunctions.

> I will give you a new heart and put a new spirit within you; I will take the heart of stone out of your flesh and give you a heart of flesh.
>
> —Ezekiel 36:26

Closed and Unable to Receive

When a vessel is closed, it cannot receive anything. An empty bucket can be set outside in a rainstorm, yet that empty bucket will not be filled with water if it is covered with a lid. Possibly, in the past, you have experienced the outpouring of God's Spirit upon your life, but because you were unwilling to take off your "lid," you were unable to receive the benefits of that outpouring.

You cannot receive from the Lord if your lid is tightly in place, completely closed off to the work of the Holy Spirit. You will receive from God only if you "open up."

Just as the man with the withered hand was asked by Jesus to stretch forth his hand (Matt. 12:13), Jesus is asking you to uncover and expose your weaknesses. Are you willing to remove every form of self-protection (the anger, the emotional numbness, the denial, the control, etc.) and stretch forth every broken and unhealed area in your life?

Opening yourself up to reveal emotional hurt or weakness is one of life's toughest challenges. It's somewhat scary. It's not easy to "open up." More than likely, you've spent a lot of energy staying closed to protect yourself from more pain. Perhaps you've even become an expert in defense mechanisms to keep yourself closed up. Let's look at a few examples.

Perhaps you have mastered the defense mechanism of denial. Denial is subtle. You may not even be aware that you have used it to cover up your dysfunction. Possibly, you have been afraid to face your issues, so, instead, you denied their existence. You may have even convinced yourself you don't have any problems, but everyone else around you does. *They* are the real problem.

People who live in denial are blinded by their own dysfunction. But they have eagle eyes when it comes to everyone else's, causing them to be judgmental and critical of others. These are the people who feel that when the pastor is preaching a convicting message, they don't need it and say, "Amen, I hope my neighbor gets this. They really need it!"

DELUSIONAL THINKING AND EMOTIONAL NUMBNESS

Delusional thinking is another defense mechanism. If you have mastered this ability, you have convinced yourself that you are "OK" when in reality you aren't. Somehow, you see yourself as you want to be, not as you really are.

People who adopt a lifestyle of "delusional thinking" basically lie to themselves. Consequently, when others tell them the truth about how they really are, they become angry and defensive, unable to understand how anyone could accuse them of such things.

Others have mastered the defense mechanism of "emotional numbness." Perhaps, to avoid the pain you've experienced in life, you have shut down emotionally, refusing to allow yourself to feel anything. You haven't just hidden your emotions—you've banished them, choosing to live in a robot-like state emotionally!

People who ban their emotions merely "exist" in survival mode and are not living life to the fullest. They are walking-dead people, closed off to both the good and the bad. They don't really laugh. They don't enjoy things. They don't cry. They don't feel the love that others express toward them. They don't even feel God's love. They simply don't feel. And if they ever do feel, usually the only permissible emotion they allow themselves to express is anger.

At times, emotionally numb people will recite the

details of a devastating event in their lives. Most often, these details are shared in a monotone voice with a smile on their face. They may even say they are "opening up." However, sharing details and expressing emotion are two very different things. "Opening up" involves honestly expressing emotions—sharing not just what happened, but how it made them feel.

CREATED TO BE PASSIONATE

In life, everyone suffers some level of hurt, abuse, abandonment, rejection, disappointment, and failure. These wounds serve as an open door for fear to enter. When fear takes root, it becomes a stronghold that controls one's life, causing defensive behaviors of self-protection such as denial, delusional thinking, and emotional numbness. If you struggle with any one of these defensive behaviors, you are closed off to God's abundant life and you will lack passion.

Remember when you were a child, before you suffered some of life's unfair traumas? You were carefree. It was easy to cry, laugh, and smile. You were open emotionally. But as you grew up, you experienced things that hurt you, which caused you to become less and less emotional. Little by little, you lost passion.

Jesus was passionate about everything He did. He prayed passionately (Luke 22:44). He loved passionately (John 15:13). He expressed emotion passionately! He wept (John 11:35). He demonstrated so much joy He was accused of being a wine-bibber (Luke 7:34). He displayed righteous anger when He overturned the tables in the temple (Matt. 21:12–13). He was compassionate, moved

Getting Started

with deep love for those in need (Mark 6:34). He grieved, as seen in the Garden of Gethsemane when He prayed with such intensity that His sweat became like drops of blood (Luke 22:44).

Jesus was passionate in life and in death. He was passionate as He prayed, "O My Father, if this cup cannot pass away from Me unless I drink it, Your will be done" (Matt. 26:42). He was passionate when He cried out on the cross, "My God, My God, why have You forsaken Me?" (Matt. 27:46).

We were created by God to be passionate. He is a passionate God (Deut. 4:24), and we are created in His image (Gen. 1:27). He wants us to be full of passion because the more passionate we are, the closer He can come to us. If you feel as though you have lost your passion and want it to be restored, you must be willing to surrender to the healing process and open your heart to receive.

> The sacrifices of God are a broken spirit, a broken and a contrite heart—these, O God, You will not despise.
> —PSALM 51:17

BROKENNESS: THE PROCESS TO OPENNESS

Have you ever struggled to open a brand-new jar of something in your pantry? Regardless of how strong your grip is or how you grasp the lid, it just won't budge!

When a jar is sealed shut, nothing can be poured out and nothing can be poured in. The outside of the jar can be touched, but the inside remains untouchable until the jar is opened. The process of opening the jar begins with the breaking of the seal. Once the seal is broken, the lid to the jar is loosened and can then be easily removed, allowing access to the jar's interior.

This simple example depicts our heart. Unless our heart is open, it is unable to receive anything from the Lord. What is in our heart remains untouched. For this reason, the Holy Spirit moves upon our heart to bring us to a place of brokenness. But, because we most often misunderstand this process, we violently fight against it, not realizing we are fighting against the plan of God to open us up so we can receive His healing.

Brokenness is the will of God for your life. "The sacrifices of God are a broken spirit, a broken and a contrite heart—these, O God, You will not despise" (Ps. 51:17). It is this sacrifice that pleases God.

Right now, you might be asking, "How can it please God if I'm all broken up and a mess?"

What Is Brokenness?

To help you better understand, let's define brokenness— what it is and what it is not. First of all, brokenness is not devastation. It is possible to be totally devastated without being broken. Many have experienced devastating circumstances, and instead of being broken, they've become bitter and even more closed off. Even though their lives are shattered into millions of pieces, they respond with toughness and shut down emotionally.

So what is brokenness? Brokenness is complete surrender, yielding our will to His will.[1] It is praying, "Not [my] will, but Yours," and meaning it (Luke 22:42). It is the act of giving up control. It is the act of letting go. Brokenness is total dependence upon the Lord, knowing that without Him we can do nothing (John 15:5). It is complete trust in God that is not swayed by what we feel or by what we are going through. Brokenness says, "God, I may not understand, but I will not fear. I will trust You and You alone." (See Proverbs 3:5–6.)

Brokenness is evidenced by an attitude of repentance, which brings a change of heart. "So produce fruit that is consistent with repentance [demonstrating new behavior that proves a change of heart, and a conscious decision to turn away from sin]" (Matt. 3:8 AMP). If a person has difficulty admitting their shortcomings, they are not broken. Whenever someone is walking in brokenness, they are quick to accept responsibility for their offenses and readily repent without blaming others. Their repentance bears the fruit of a changed heart.

Brokenness is evidenced by an attitude of humility. "Humble yourselves under the mighty hand of God, that He may exalt you in due time" (1 Pet. 5:6). Therefore, if a person is arrogant and prideful, they are not broken. A person walking in brokenness humbles themself under the mighty hand of God, knowing that they can do nothing in and of themself. They are totally dependent upon the Lord.

Brokenness is evidenced by sensitivity and softness. A person walking in brokenness will be kind, tenderhearted, compassionate, merciful, loving, and forgiving. When a person is hardhearted, they are not broken. They have not allowed the Lord to remove their heart of stone and give them a heart of flesh.

> I will give you a new heart and put a new spirit within you; I will take the heart of stone out of your flesh and give you a heart of flesh.
> —Ezekiel 36:26

Open Your Vessel to Receive

Brokenness is the key. It is the process that opens our vessel to receive. It is not an easy process, but it is the only process that will open us up. We cannot go through this process in our own strength. It's painful. It's too much for us, which is why we have perfected methods of self-protection such as denial, delusional thinking, and emotional numbness. We need the help of the Holy Spirit, the Spirit of Truth, to help us open up. Once we are open, the healing process can begin!

> But when the Helper comes, whom I shall send to you from the Father, the Spirit of truth who proceeds from the Father, He will testify of Me.
> —John 15:26

To help illustrate how the Holy Spirit brings truth into our hearts to open us up, I want to share a powerful testimony from a woman in our congregation.

As a young child, this woman suffered abuse that left her with more emotional pain than she was able to handle. She began stuffing the pain inside and denying its existence. In her adult life, she was diagnosed with fibromyalgia. The pain was so excruciating that the doctors prescribed narcotic pain medication, yet she felt no relief. She was in physical pain nearly every day of her life for over ten years.

One day, she attended a special service at our church. During the service, I preached a message entitled, "What's Keeping You from Sonship?" During the message, the Holy Spirit revealed to her that she needed to be set free from the emotional damage and abuse she suffered as a young child. When she came forward for prayer, the moment hands were laid on her, the emotional pain locked inside was emptied out through gut-wrenching tears. Her cry was painful and uncontrollable. But when the emotional pain was emptied out, so was the physical pain. She has not suffered from fibromyalgia since! She is free to walk in sonship and fulfill the call of God upon her life.

For thirty-eight years, this woman lived in denial, seemingly protecting herself from the painful memories of abuse. She suffered physical illness, not knowing the root cause. But as she heard the Word, the Holy Spirit opened up her eyes and revealed truth to her spirit, exposing the root of her dysfunction. If she wanted to be free, she would have to open up her heart, empty out the pain, and allow the healing process to take place. Even though it was a painful process, one she greatly feared, it brought her permanent relief.

The Truth

> And you shall know the truth, and the truth shall make you free.
> —John 8:32

Truth is God's powerful liberating force. Without truth, there is no freedom. It sounds simple, but it isn't.

In our humanness, we are afraid of the truth because it is most often painful. Thus, we oppose the very thing that can loose us.

One of the hardest truths to face is abuse by family members. This is especially true of parents. Unfortunately, there are no perfect parents. Even though they may not have meant to hurt us, they did. We most often resist facing this truth. Why? We love them and we desperately need their love. We do not want to risk losing their affection. While we are aware that there are no perfect parents, they are the only parents we have. We don't want to be disloyal to them. We want to keep the family peace.

Possibly, you have been afraid of the truth, and you've worn a mask with a fake smile, pretending that you have been OK when you're really not OK. You've run from the truth instead of embracing it. Are you willing to stop running? Are you willing to allow the Holy Spirit to reveal truth and make you free?

The pages of this book would not allow the space necessary to uncover all the truths that need to be revealed in your life. But I would like to discuss one that I believe tends to be the most prevalent in people's lives—the father wound.

As you continue reading, please pray and ask the Holy Spirit to expose the root of your dysfunction. He knows you better than you know yourself. He is the Spirit of Truth.

THE FATHER WOUND

Many suffer from what is commonly referred to as a *father wound*. Simply defined, a father wound is a hurt that is caused by a father figure. Often these wounds are unintentional. At times, however, these wounds are blatant, intentional actions. This hurt comes in many forms: abandonment, rejection, conditional love, neglect, violence, physical abuse, verbal abuse, emotional abuse, sexual abuse, and more. The wounds inflicted by these hurts are most devastating to the emotional well-being and security of a child.

When there is an absence of constant, healthy, affirming love from a father, the child suffers emotional damage that affects their sense of belonging, their sense of worth and value, and their sense of being competent. The child grows up feeling unloved, unwanted, unaccepted, rejected, fearful, empty, lonely, uncared for, devalued, worthless, inferior, incompetent, insecure, guilty, shameful, angry, and unable to succeed. Whether male or female, every child needs the love and affirmation of a father and will greatly suffer without it.

Humankind's need for a father is so near to the heart of God that He has identified Himself as our heavenly Father. He demonstrated just how important His love as a Father is when He affirmed and validated Jesus before Jesus' ministry began. In Matthew 3:17, Jesus heard the words spoken by His Father that all children desire to hear: "This is My beloved Son, in whom I am well pleased." These were empowering words from the Father to His Son at a pivotal point in Jesus' life.

Every child needs the same kind of blessing from

their natural father. Sadly, due to the natural father's own dysfunction and ignorance, he often fails to bestow this kind of love and affirmation on his child. This lack often results in a young man or woman growing into adulthood questioning their own worth and place in life. When this need is not met in God's ordained way, the child ends up seeking to meet this need in unhealthy ways. This is one of the main reasons why many young people fall into a life of sin, drugs, alcohol, and promiscuity. Perhaps they start running with the wrong crowd. All they are really doing is trying to find validation and acceptance in something or someone because they've not received it from their natural father.

Unfortunately, father wounds do not just affect people in their youth. If these wounds are not properly healed, they will affect them throughout their entire lives. For this reason, many grown men are insecure with no understanding of their identity. Many grown women go from one unhealthy relationship to another, seeking someone who will make them feel loved and valued. The effects of the father wound are profound and long-lasting.

I feel for those who have this type of validation missing from their lives. However, there is hope. This affirmation may never come from your natural father. But your heavenly Father is waiting with open arms to freely give this kind of love and acceptance to you today. Do not allow your perception of your natural father to become your perception of your heavenly Father.

Your loving heavenly Father will never fail you. He will never reject or abandon you. Hear His word today:

"You are My son (or daughter). I love you and I am pleased with you. I accept you and validate you."

Even though I have been specifically discussing the issue of a father wound, it is possible that other types of wounds can come from a mother, bringing significant hurt and damage. These wounds, from either parent, produce an atmosphere of instability and insecurity that will accompany you throughout your life until you deal with it.

Please understand that when your parent hurts you, it is usually because of their own dysfunction. Even though their actions are directed at you, they are not about you.

> YOUR LOVING HEAVENLY FATHER WILL NEVER FAIL YOU.

Your parent is hurting from their past, and hurting people hurt people.

You will never be able to fix your parents or go back in time to erase the past. The only power you have is over your own life. Your parents may never ask for forgiveness. But that does not mean you are excused from giving it. Unforgiveness only affects and damages your life.

So it is time to take responsibility for your own life. Do not allow yourself to be controlled by the mistakes and shortcomings of your parents.

It is time to grow beyond the hurt of your past.

FORGIVENESS

I want to remind you of a biblical perspective on forgiveness. In 1 Samuel, we read that David was a servant to King Saul. But Saul was more than just a king to David; he was also a father figure. If anyone ever had a right to be hurt by a father wound, it was David. Saul was unfair, abusive, and malicious. His mistreatment of David became so severe that he literally sought to kill him.

> Then Saul sought to pin David to the wall with the spear, but he slipped away from Saul's presence; and he drove the spear into the wall. So David fled and escaped that night.
> —1 SAMUEL 19:10

In 1 Samuel 18:11, we read that Saul had already attempted to take David's life by hurling a spear at him. "And Saul cast the spear, for he said, 'I will pin David to the wall!' But David escaped his presence twice."

There is a revelation in this story that is of great significance. When someone you love hurts you, do not let it stick to you. Do not allow the abuse, the hurtful words, and the rejection to penetrate your heart. Let them stick to the wall as Saul's spear did.

Will those actions hurt and disturb you? Yes. But do not let them become attached to you, defining or damaging you. Please understand that when someone hurts you, it is more of a reflection of them than it is of you. Let me explain. You are not the reason they are abusive, angry, and cruel. Those behaviors are an indication of something wrong in the character of the one committing those actions. Even though their actions are directed at you, it is not about you. It is a result of their bondage and dysfunction. When you realize this, compassion can grow in your heart toward them, and you will find it possible to forgive.

Saul's abuse and mistreatment of David was relentless.

Yet David walked in forgiveness. This is underscored in 1 Samuel 24. David was given an opportunity to take Saul's life. He was given the chance to do to Saul what Saul had tried numerous times to do to him.

> Then the men of David said to him, "This is the day of which the LORD said to you, 'Behold, I will deliver your enemy into your hand, that you may do to him as it seems good to you.'" And David arose and secretly cut off a corner of Saul's robe.
> —1 SAMUEL 24:4

David secretly cut the skirt of Saul while he was resting in a cave. After doing so, verse 5 tells us that David's heart smote him.

> Now it happened afterward that David's heart troubled him because he had cut Saul's robe.
> —1 SAMUEL 24:5

At that moment, David decided not to allow Saul's sin to become his sin. Saul was murderous. Had David killed Saul, he, too, would have become murderous. Instead, through forgiveness, he released Saul into God's hands.

FORGIVENESS BREAKS THE CYCLE

Forgiveness is important for many reasons. First, it is a biblical command (Matt. 6:14–15). However, there is more to it than just that. Forgiveness is the one thing that destroys iniquity and generational curses, breaking the cycle.

For example, many people who had alcoholic fathers

grow up and become alcoholics themselves. Others who were raised in an abusive home grow up and become abusive. Why? How could those who have been hurt so deeply by these behaviors grow up and fall into the same trap? The answer is simple: unforgiveness.

How about you? Has your parents' sin become your sin? Are you bound by generational curses and iniquity? David stopped that cycle by simply allowing forgiveness into his heart. If you truly want to destroy iniquity and generational curses, forgive. Forgiveness will destroy that root forever!

Isn't It Time to Let Go?

Isn't it time to let go and forgive? Isn't it time to release those who hurt you into God's hands?

David had victory over a lion, a bear, and a giant. But none of these victories released him into his destiny.

So what did? It was forgiveness. The day he forgave Saul was his greatest victory! This is when he stepped into his destiny.

Over the years, I've seen many people become frustrated because they have been unable to realize the fullness of God's destiny in their lives. Perhaps He is waiting for them to pass the test of forgiveness.

How about you? Are you frustrated and seemingly unable to step into your destiny? If you walk in forgiveness, God will withhold nothing from you. It's time to forgive.

PRAYER

Dear Jesus, I know that forgiveness is a gift—a gift that is a result of Your grace. No one deserves it, including me. I have needed and will continue to need it in my life; therefore, I choose to walk in forgiveness toward others. Just as David defeated the giant of unforgiveness, so will I. I know that destiny is waiting for me on the other side! I choose to release. I choose to forgive. In Your name I pray, amen.

Chapter 19

A CLOSER LOOK AT FORGIVENESS

UNFORGIVENESS IS THE enemy's strongest and most effective trap. Why? Because a snare is a trap that tightens its grip the more you try to get free. It's impossible to loose yourself. Proverbs describes it like this: "It is harder to win back the friendship of an offended brother than to capture a fortified city. His anger shuts you out like iron bars" (Prov. 18:19, TLB).

Scripture tells us that offenses are inevitable: "It is impossible that no offenses should come" (Luke 17:1). We live in this fallen world, and no one is immune from hurt. People will mistreat you, abuse you, betray you, abandon you, reject you, lie about you, etc. No one is immune.

The word "offense" comes from the Greek word *skandalon*, which means snare.[1] When an offense comes your way, it snares you and traps you in unforgiveness, holding you captive to pain and hurt.

Unforgiveness is a Progressive Disease

Unforgiveness begins with an injury. It comes from people who are closest to us, the ones we love the most—parents, husbands, wives, children, best friends. It comes from people who are compulsive—they don't mean to hurt us, but they can't control themselves. It comes from people who are hurting. Remember, hurting people hurt people. Their pain spills over onto innocent bystanders. Hurt even comes from people with good intentions who, despite their best efforts, fail us. It comes from human beings—imperfect, broken, and flawed. Some hurt us by disloyalty, violating our trust, betraying us, abandoning us, rejecting us. Others hurt us through violence, abuse, and sin.

Hurt always causes pain. When pain is left untreated, infection sets in. That infection produces a fast-growing malignancy called bitterness. Bitterness eats away at our joy, our peace, our strength, our life, and our ability to love and be loved.

But bitterness doesn't just hurt you—it hurts others:

> Watch out that no bitterness takes root among you, for as it springs up it causes deep trouble, hurting many in their spiritual lives.
> —HEBREWS 12:15, TLB

Everything that comes out of bitter people is tainted. Their bitterness takes over, controlling their actions, behaviors, attitudes, emotions, and decisions, destroying their ability to produce good fruit.

Bitterness manifests in many ways, but I want to focus on three specific evidences of bitterness:

First, bitter people tend to be angry people. They feel entitled to their anger. They believe they have been wronged and they have a right to act out. After all, it's not their fault. Their anger is expressed through violence, cruel words, harshness, judgments, revenge, hatred, controlling behaviors, and a lack of mercy and compassion. But sometimes this anger is not the in-your-face kind. It's passive. It seeps out in sarcasm, snide remarks, put-downs, and cruel jokes. Other times their anger is turned inward, manifesting as depression, addictions, self-hatred, and self-destructive behaviors.

Second, bitter people tend to be easily offended people. Because their wounds remain unhealed, they are still in pain, causing them to be on guard. They live in a defensive posture, ready to pounce at the slightest offense. Maybe you looked at them wrong. Maybe you didn't spend enough time with them. Maybe you failed to show appreciation the way they expected. Most often, because unforgiveness distorts perception, they see things that aren't there or they don't see things that are. They carry a "victim" mentality, feeling like everyone is out to get them.

They see themselves as helpless victims and tend to feel paranoid, suspicious, unloved, unappreciated, unaccepted, rejected, jealous, used, and abused. They carry a chip on their shoulder, and no matter how much someone loves them, blesses them, or compliments them, it's never enough to make them happy.

Eventually, easily offended people find themselves alone and isolated. No matter how many relationships they enter, their circle of friends keeps getting smaller. As their world shrinks, they find someone who is mad at the same people they are mad at. But eventually, even that person turns against them—until finally, they are sitting in a room all alone—*mad*.

In this condition, the easily offended person loses the

ability to bond with others, even though they desperately need relationships. They drive away anyone who tries to get close.

Third, bitter people tend to be tormented people.

In Matthew 18, Jesus tells the story of a man who was forgiven a massive debt yet refused to forgive someone who owed him a much smaller amount. His unforgiveness gave the enemy a legal right to come into his life and deliver him to the tormentors.

> And his master was angry, and delivered him to the torturers until he should pay all that was due to him. So My heavenly Father also will do to you if each of you, from his heart, does not forgive his brother his trespasses.
> —MATTHEW 18:34–35

Bitter people can't escape what happened to them. They replay it over and over in their minds, miserable and consumed by tormenting thoughts. The more they dwell on it, the angrier and unhappier they become. They can't sleep, and when they do, they dream about it. Their minds are eaten up with hatred, plotting ways to exact revenge.

Unforgiveness binds them to the sin of the one who hurt them. Then the very thing that hurt them they can't help but repeat themselves.

DO UNFORGIVENESS AND BITTERNESS CAUSE PHYSICAL ILLNESS?

Scientific research increasingly affirms what Scripture has long revealed—our thought life and emotions directly impact our physical health. While studies vary, some researchers estimate that as much as 87 percent of all illnesses can be traced back to toxic emotions, while only 13 percent are linked to diet, genetics, and environmental factors.[2]

Please understand, I am not saying all physical illnesses are caused by unforgiveness. But there is no denying that unforgiveness negatively affects our health. Over the years I have witnessed people receive healing from arthritis, migraines, cardiovascular issues, immune deficiencies, and even cancer when they finally chose to walk in forgiveness.

> IF YOU SUFFER FROM UNFORGIVENESS, I HAVE GOOD NEWS—YOU DON'T HAVE TO SUFFER ANYMORE!

If you suffer from unforgiveness, I have good news—you don't have to suffer anymore!

Your pain, misery, and torment can end.

It's curable.

What's the cure? Forgiveness.

Forgiveness is the only cure.

THINGS YOU NEED TO KNOW ABOUT FORGIVENESS

1. Forgiveness is not an option.

Forgiveness is not optional. The message of the cross is clear—it's a message of perfect and complete forgiveness.

> For if you forgive men their trespasses, your heavenly Father will also forgive you. But if you do

not forgive men their trespasses, neither will your Father forgive your trespasses.
—Matthew 6:14–15

On the cross, Jesus paid the price for your sins. Yes, I said your sins. As a human being, you are not perfect. You make mistakes. You mess up. At times, you say or do the wrong thing. You hurt others. You sin. The Bible says, "All have sinned" (Rom. 3:23), and that includes you. You need forgiveness, and without it, you are not going to heaven. Your eternal destiny hangs in the balance.

It is difficult to forgive others. It is even more difficult when you fail to see your own need for forgiveness. Please realize you will not always be the "victim" of other people's mistreatment. Every so often, whether you mean to or not, you will inflict pain on somebody else, and you will need their forgiveness.

God's Word is very clear. You need forgiveness. However, for you to receive it, you must give it. You must sow forgiveness to reap forgiveness. It's very simple:

If you forgive, you are forgiven.

But if you don't forgive, you are not forgiven (Matt. 6:14–15).

Unforgiveness is a sin, and if you hold on to it, you cannot be forgiven.

When Jesus was paying the price for your sins on the cross, at the same time, He was also paying the price for the sins of every person who has ever or ever will hurt you.

As He has forgiven you, you must forgive others.

2. No one deserves forgiveness.

You don't deserve to be forgiven, and neither does anyone who has hurt you. You deserve to be punished for your sins. Those who have hurt you deserve to be punished for their sins.

But God's forgiveness is not based on what is or is not deserved. If it were, all of humankind would be in big trouble, for we are all unworthy of His forgiveness!

His forgiveness is based solely upon Himself. Forgiveness is a result of His grace, giving you a gift that you did not deserve! Forgiveness is the result of His mercy. In mercy, Jesus took upon Himself your punishment and the punishment for every person who has ever wounded you.

When forgiving others, remember, forgiveness is not based on those who have hurt you. They don't deserve forgiveness. Don't try to find a reason to forgive them, because you may not find one.

Forgiveness is an undeserved gift!

3. For you to forgive, it is not necessary for the offender to repent.

Forgiveness would be so much easier if those who have offended you would come to you and say, "I did you wrong. I'm sorry. Would you forgive me?" Sadly, some people will never repent and will never ask for forgiveness. Not only will they not ask, but they also feel they did nothing wrong. So they continue in their hurtful behaviors.

Whether they ask or not, you still have a responsibility to forgive them. You don't need their cooperation to forgive. You don't even have to talk to them to forgive them. In some cases, it may be dangerous to communicate with them because doing so could put you in harm's way. You don't need to send them a letter, make a phone call, or hear an apology to forgive.

All you need is the presence of Jesus to help you.

4. There is a difference between forgiveness and restoration.

You don't need someone's cooperation to forgive them, but you must have their cooperation to restore your relationship with them.

For example, if someone has physically abused you, you need to forgive them. However, you can forgive them without keeping them in your house where they can continue to abuse you. Restoration is not the same as forgiveness. Restoration should come only as a result of genuine repentance.

When someone truly repents...

- They acknowledge that what they did was wrong—without blaming you or someone else for their bad behavior.

- They are remorseful.

- They have a change of heart, seeking God's help to never repeat their hurtful actions again.

- They demonstrate the fruit of repentance, which is evidence of their changed heart (Matt. 3:8).

- Then, and only then, should they be restored into a place of relationship in your life.

Perhaps you have had a misperception, thinking that restoration and forgiveness are the same. If so, this misunderstanding has likely caused you to jump back into relationships with those who have not repented, resulting in you being hurt over and over again.

Until someone repents, they are like a hot stove— if you touch it, you will get burned. It's unwise and even dangerous to go back into abusive and unhealthy relationships.

Forgiveness releases you from being tied to someone. In forgiveness, you let them go, knowing that until they repent, you are released from relationship with them.

- You should not continue doing business with them.
- You should not call them on the phone and pretend all is well.
- You should not go to lunch together.
- You should not invite them over to your house.
- You should not allow them into your inner circle.

Even though the prodigal son's father never held anything against him, the son was not restored until he repented (Luke 15:18–24).

Yet the father was open to restoration—as soon as the

son left, he started feeding the calf and looking in the direction of where his son had gone. He was ready to receive him back. However, the son could not be restored to his position until he stood up and said, "I will arise and go to my father, and will say to him, 'Father, I have sinned...'" (Luke 15:18).

I also think it is important to note that forgiveness is not the same as trust. Because you forgive someone, it does not mean you should trust them. If you had an employee who stole cash from the register, you have a responsibility to forgive them, but it doesn't mean you should trust them to continue running your cash register.

Forgiveness does not mean there are no consequences or repercussions. It does not mean you have to lie down and be a doormat, allowing people to treat you badly or take advantage of you.

There is a big difference between forgiveness and restoration, and it is critical to understand that difference.

5. Forgiveness does not mean forgetting.

God is the only One capable of forgiving and forgetting. You don't have that ability, and God is not going to give you amnesia! You can't forgive what you don't remember. If you don't remember, there's nothing to forgive. The human mind is highly efficient in remembering wrongs. You need to forgive because your memory keeps the pain alive long after the actual offense occurred.

The miracle of forgiveness is that through the help of the Holy Spirit, you are able to forgive even while remembering what someone did to hurt you. Forgiveness does not mean forgetting. But it does change your perception of how you "see" the past. Instead of seeing someone as a wicked person who hurt you, you begin to see them as a human being with dysfunction who needs help.

6. Forgiveness is a choice, not a feeling.

Often I have heard people say that they do not feel like they can forgive because their pain is just too great. But forgiveness has nothing to do with emotions. If we wait until we "feel" like forgiving, we probably never will.

Forgiveness is not about feelings; it is a choice. It is a conscious decision that says, "No matter how much I hurt, I choose to forgive. Whether they deserve it or not, I choose to forgive. Whether they repent or not, I choose to forgive. I choose to release them from the debt they owe me. I choose to release them into the hand of God. I choose forgiveness."

> FORGIVENESS DOES MORE THAN FREE THE ONE WHO WRONGED YOU—IT FREES YOU.

7. Forgiveness is the only remedy for your pain.

Forgiveness is not easy, particularly because of the emotional pain that accompanies being hurt. But forgiveness does not ignore your pain—it confronts it and brings relief. It is the only remedy for the pain caused by hurt. You will never be free from what someone did to wound you unless you choose to forgive.

Forgiveness does more than free the one who wronged you—it frees you. It releases you from being the "victim" and causes you to become the "victor"! It breaks the chains of victimization that have kept you bound.

The Greek word for "forgiving" comes from the root word *chairó*, which means to be cheerful, happy, joyful, and made well.[3] Forgiveness restores your joy. Haven't you been miserable long enough? Choosing to forgive will allow joy to flood your soul once again. All the poison and toxins will be emptied out, and you will be made whole.

Fear

Fear is one of the primary driving forces of dysfunctional behavior. It fuels control, deception, and manipulation. People lash out in anger and abuse others because they are afraid. They lie to avoid rejection. They act arrogant and prideful to mask insecurity. They shut down emotionally, unable to bond with others, all because of fear. These self-protective behaviors are all a result of fear.

Whenever we are hurt, it opens the door for fear to take root in our lives. Unhealed wounds invite fear to dominate us. If we give place to that fear, we begin to build walls of self-protection that keep us trapped inside. But living in fear is not living at all. It's bondage. Instead of being controlled by the past hurt of another, fear forces you to relive that pain over and over.

> For God has not given us a spirit of fear, but of power and of love and of a sound mind.
> —2 Timothy 1:7

Allow me to clarify something. Not all fear is bad. The fear of touching a hot stove, falling asleep while driving, or failing to pay your rent on time are examples of protective, healthy fear. This kind of fear serves a purpose—it protects us. If you're afraid of being evicted, pay your rent on time. If you don't want to get burned, don't touch a hot stove. Healthy fear keeps you from harm.

However, there is another kind of fear—the kind the enemy brings. This fear is never based on wisdom, common sense, or the Word of God. It is fueled by past experiences, painful betrayals, and a long history of disappointments. It's important to discern when you are under the influence of godly fear versus demonic fear. Godly fear brings a deep, settling peace. Demonic fear brings anxiety, unrest, and torment. One protects you from harm; the other keeps you from the good that God has for you!

Fear Is a Spirit

Second Timothy 1:7 tells us that fear is not just an emotion—it is a spirit. And it is not a spirit sent from God. When we give place to the spirit of fear, we are allowing something into our lives that is not from Him. Living a life dominated by fear cannot be justified. Being hurt is not a valid reason to let fear take control. Fear is not just something that happens to you—it is something you allow. You cannot repent for what someone else has done to you, but you are accountable for what you have allowed fear to do in your life.

You alone must choose whether or not fear will dictate your decisions, control your behavior, or affect your relationships. No one else can make that decision for you. Only you can choose to function in life free from the influence of fear.

You may ask, "How do I stop fear from controlling my life? How can I be free?" I have three answers for you: Forgive, repent, and be filled with God's love. First, forgive those who hurt you, closing the open door that allowed fear to take root. Second, repent for permitting fear to have dominion in your life. And finally, be filled with the love of God. His love is perfect, and where it reigns, fear has no place!

> There is no fear in love; but perfect love casts out fear, because fear involves torment. But he who fears has not been made perfect in love.
> —1 John 4:18

Where fear is present, God's love is absent. But understand this—there is no lack of God's love for you. If you are experiencing an absence of His love in your life, it is not because He has withheld it. It is because you have not received it.

There have been times in my life when I desperately needed His love, yet I shut Him out. I pushed Him away, refusing to let His love penetrate my heart. And in those moments, fear overwhelmed me. Fear had taken over because I had unknowingly rejected the very thing that could set me free—His love.

> And we have known and believed the love that God has for us. God is love, and he who abides in love abides in God, and God in him.
> —1 John 4:16

Look at that phrase: "We have known and believed the love that God has for us." There is only one way to truly know God's love—you must experience it. But for that to happen, you have to open your heart, accept it, and receive it.

LET GOD LOVE YOU

Is the door to your heart closed? If so, what's stopping you from opening it and allowing Him to love you?

Is it because you didn't receive the love you needed as a child from your parents, and now you're afraid God will not love you either? Is it because you were wounded by the conditional love of an imperfect person? Is it because someone abandoned or rejected you? Do you feel unworthy of love? Is it because you've messed up, and now guilt and shame keep you trapped?

Maybe you learned you were the result of an unwanted pregnancy. Maybe you suffered years of verbal, physical, or emotional abuse at the hands of an alcoholic father. Perhaps a trusted family member violated your innocence. Maybe your spouse had an affair that ended your marriage. Regardless of the hurt you've suffered, the question remains: Why have you closed your heart to the love of God?

We live in a fallen world, and hurt is unavoidable. But the real question is, Have you allowed that hurt to make you afraid to bond, keeping you from getting close to anyone? If so, you've also shut out your heavenly Father. You need to make a conscious decision to open your heart and let Him love you.

Yes, people have wronged you. No, they should not

have done what they did. You did not deserve it. It was cruel, it was unjust, and it was sin. But hear me: You do not have to continue being a victim of their sin. Forgiveness releases you from victimization!

There are no perfect parents. No perfect families. No perfect friends. No perfect people. Human love is flawed and will fail you because it is inadequate to fill your need for love. The only love that is adequate is the perfect love of God.

So be honest with yourself. If God's love feels absent in your life, is it because you have allowed past hurts and injuries to close your heart off from Him? If so, this can all change today. It's time to take responsibility for the choice to reject His love and repent. Through repentance, your closed heart will be opened, and His love will flood your soul.

THE POWER OF GOD'S LOVE

God's love is the most powerful force on earth. It is stronger than wealth, greater than influence, and more potent than nuclear power. It is even greater than hatred. God's love is so powerful that it cannot fail!

His love is the only force that can truly transform a sinner's life. It softens a bitter soul and makes it sweet. It melts a heart filled with hatred and makes it kind and tender. His love changes a selfish, hardened person into someone generous, loving, and whole. His love heals broken hearts. His love sets the captive free. His love forgives. His love makes us whole!

The love of God is everlasting. It is sacrificial. It is filled with grace and mercy. It is amazing, unconditional, and perfect. It is beyond description and human comprehension. "God is love" (1 John 4:8). It's not just something He does—it is who He is!

The world uses the word "love" so cheaply, reducing it to a mere feeling of fondness or affection. But true love—the love of God—is not just an emotion. It is the very essence, the complete source, the substance of who He is! To understand love, we must know the Source.

God loves you! This may sound simple, but the power of His eternal, unchanging, and unwavering love for you is beyond description. He proved His love for you when He sent His Son, Jesus, to die on the cross in your place. "But God demonstrates His own love toward us, in that while we were still sinners, Christ died for us" (Rom. 5:8).

Pause for a moment. Say these three powerful words aloud: "God loves me." Think about those words: God...loves...me. His love is constant. His love is trustworthy. His love is perfect. His love will heal you and make you whole. It is the most powerful healing force in the universe.

THE APOSTLE PAUL'S PRAYER FOR THE EPHESIANS

> For this reason I bow my knees to the Father of our Lord Jesus Christ, from whom the whole family in heaven and earth is named, that He would grant you, according to the riches of His glory, to be strengthened with might through His Spirit in the inner man, that Christ may dwell in your hearts through faith; that you, being rooted and grounded in love, may be able to comprehend

with all the saints what is the width and length and depth and height—to know the love of Christ which passes knowledge; that you may be filled with all the fullness of God.
—EPHESIANS 3:14–19

The apostle Paul understood the importance of experiencing and fully grasping God's love. That's why, in his prayer for the believers in Ephesus, his central focus was on love. He didn't pray for them to have more power, to perform greater miracles, or to wield more authority over the devil. Instead, he prayed that they would be deeply rooted and firmly grounded in God's love. He passionately asked the Lord to give them revelation and understanding of the vastness of His love so they could truly know it—and be completely filled by it.

The Amplified Bible expands on this powerful prayer:

[That you may come] to know [practically, through personal experience] the love of Christ which far surpasses [mere] knowledge [without experience], that you may be filled up [throughout your being] to all the fullness of God [so that you may have the richest experience of God's presence in your lives, completely filled and flooded with God Himself]!
—EPHESIANS 3:19, AMP

What a prayer! This is my prayer for you. As you open your heart and receive God's love, healing will flow into your life. His love is the answer! Whether you are struggling with shame, guilt, condemnation, or any other bondage, His love is the only cure. There is healing power in His love—let Him make you whole!

STEP INTO HEALING

Your journey to healing begins the moment you let go of your self-protection and allow the Holy Spirit to reveal His truth to your heart. Right now, make the decision to surrender everything to God—your fears, your insecurities, your unforgiveness, your bondage, and every painful memory of the past. Place your full trust in Him and lean on His strength.

Freedom comes through repentance and forgiveness. As you release those who have hurt you from the prison of your unforgiveness, you will experience true liberty. Walk in brokenness before the Lord, allowing His love to not only heal you but also flow through you to others.

Today is your day for healing. Healing may hurt, but when you face the pain, you step into your God-given destiny! "He heals the brokenhearted and binds up their wounds" (Ps. 147:3).

PRAYER

Heavenly Father, I declare that today is the beginning of the rest of my life! This is a new day. This is a new beginning. This is my day for healing and wholeness. I ask that from this day forward, You would help me say goodbye to the past and embrace my present and future. Thank You for helping me step into my healing. In Jesus' name, amen.

CONCLUSION

THROUGHOUT MY TIME in ministry, I have often heard it said that God will take us to such a place of healing that He will even remove our scars. But is this true? While I believe that God stops the bleeding, removes the pain, and brings complete healing to the wound, I do not believe He removes the scars.

John 20:24–28 recounts a story involving one of Jesus' disciples, Thomas. Many refer to him as "Doubting Thomas." After the resurrection of Jesus, when the other disciples told Thomas they had seen the risen Lord, he refused to believe unless he could see the scars in Christ's hands. He needed visible proof of the resurrection.

> Then He said to Thomas, "Reach your finger here, and look at My hands; and reach your hand here, and put it into My side. Do not be unbelieving, but believing."
>
> —JOHN 20:27

In John's account, Jesus gently corrected Thomas, telling him it is better to believe without seeing. But notice something significant—Jesus did not remove His scars. The scars in His hands and side remained. Why? Because our scars are what identify us to those we are called to reach.

It was Thomas—doubting Thomas—who said, "Show me the scars! I will not believe it unless I see the scars!" (paraphrased from John 20:25). Once he saw them and touched them, he fell to his knees, proclaiming, "My Lord and my God!" (John 20:28). The scars became the proof of Christ's resurrection. The very thing that once brought pain now became a testimony.

The Purpose of Your Scars

Why do scars remain? Our scars are not meant to be hidden; they serve a greater purpose. They identify us to those we are called to reach. Scars tell a story—not just of the pain we endured, but of the healing we received. They remind others that they, too, can heal.

Think about it—how can you truly reach someone who suffered sexual abuse as a child, battles a life of addiction, or is trapped in an abusive relationship if you have never faced and healed from similar wounds? Your scars speak a language that others who are hurting can understand.

Consider someone with a broken arm. If you've never broken a bone, you might have sympathy for their pain, but you can't truly empathize with their experience. You can't walk them through the pain, the healing process, or the struggle of regaining strength in the same way that someone who has endured it can. Shared experience is a powerful bridge to healing.

Your scars are not a mark of shame; they are a sign of survival. They are proof that God is a healer. The wounds may have once caused unbearable pain, but now, healed and transformed, they become a testimony of God's faithfulness.

Conclusion

SCARS QUALIFY YOU

Your pain, past, and struggles do not disqualify you from your purpose. In fact, your scars are what qualify you. They tell a story—a story of survival, healing, and transformation. People don't need to hear a sermon to know what you've been through; they can see it in your scars.

I have a scar across the top of my left hand. It serves as a constant reminder of an experience that could have been much worse. While cutting back branches from a tree, my saw slipped, slicing through the top of my hand. In pain and bleeding badly, I climbed down, jumped into my truck, and sped off to get help. Determined not to bleed all over my brand-new truck, I drove with my arm hanging out the window, which, in hindsight, was probably not the best plan!

I was young and impatient, so I didn't properly tend to the wound. A few days later, I woke up to find my entire hand and forearm swollen to twice their normal size. The wound had become infected because I ignored the need for proper healing.

There's an important lesson here: Wounds that are not treated properly will inevitably become infected. This applies to both physical and emotional wounds. Many people try to move forward without addressing the pain of their past. But unhealed wounds don't just go away—they fester beneath the surface, growing worse with time.

That infection required me to return to the doctor, where the medical staff vigorously scrubbed and cleaned the wound. The process was painful, but it was necessary for healing. Sometimes we need additional help to heal.

The same is true for emotional and spiritual wounds. If we don't allow God, our Great Physician, to cleanse and heal the pain of our past, it will remain infected, affecting every area of our lives. But when God heals, He heals completely.

Today, I no longer have a wound—only a scar. A scar is a reminder of what I went through, but the pain is no longer there. I can tell the story of my injury without reliving the suffering.

This story has found its way into so many sermons, counseling sessions, and conversations. Some people laugh when they picture me climbing down a tree, bleeding, and frantically trying to save my truck from the mess. Others have been moved to tears as they recognize their own emotional wounds that have been left untreated for far too long.

Your scars are not a sign of weakness; they are proof of healing. Let God heal the wounds, so that one day, you can share your scars as a testimony of His faithfulness.

Scars Testify of Healing

Here's the best thing about scars—they are not wounds. They are evidence that the wound once existed but has now healed.

Scars don't tell the story of pain; they tell the story of victory. They are a reminder that, yes, you were hurt, but you are no longer hurting. You may have bled, but you are no longer bleeding. You may have suffered, but you survived.

Your scars are proof that healing is possible. They testify that you have overcome what was meant to break you. They speak not of defeat but of resilience. They show that you walked through the fire and came out refined, not consumed.

So don't hide your scars. Instead, let them be a testimony. Let them be a beacon of hope for those still hurting, a reminder that God is faithful to heal, restore, and redeem. You are not the same person you were when you were wounded—you are bigger, better, and stronger!

Don't Hide Your Scars!

Don't hide your scars! Let's go back to the story of Thomas. The first thing Jesus did when He entered the room was go straight to Thomas and tell him to see and touch His scars for himself. "Then He said to Thomas, 'Reach your finger here, and look at My hands; and reach your hand here, and put it into My side. Do not be unbelieving, but believing'" (John 20:27). This moment speaks a powerful truth to us—not only should we allow people to see our pain, but we should also allow them to feel it.

We should live in such a place of self-awareness, transparency, and integrity that when we talk about our pain, it's not just words—it's real. People shouldn't just hear our stories; they should feel the transformation behind them. It's not enough to just discuss details—we must be open about the emotions behind them. That is openness. That is what being real is all about.

Just as the scars on Jesus' hands identified Him to His disciple Thomas, your scars will identify you to those

> **Don't hide your scars!**

you are called to reach. We all know people who are looking to us for answers—people who need hope and are searching for someone who has been where they are and made it through. Don't hide your scars! We should never be ashamed of them. They serve as a testament to the sovereign work of God in our lives.

If the scars weren't removed from Jesus, why would they be removed from you? A friend once told me, "We need to bring our wounds to Jesus, let Him heal them, and use our scars for His glory." Your scars are trophies of what God has done in your life, giving hope to others who are still hurting!

Now, it is my prayer that you begin to walk in healing, destiny, and abundant life! It is time for God to turn what the enemy meant for evil into good! "But as for you, you meant evil against me; but God meant it for good" (Gen. 50:20). It is time for you to turn your scars into testimonies. It is time for you to be who God has called you to be.

> WE NEED TO BRING OUR WOUNDS TO JESUS, LET HIM HEAL THEM, AND USE OUR SCARS FOR HIS GLORY.

You deserve healing. You deserve freedom. Give yourself permission to fight for what is yours. Healing hurts, but staying hurt hurts worse. Embrace the process, step into abundant life, and walk boldly in your God-given destiny.

It's now or never!

A PERSONAL INVITATION TO KNOW JESUS

GOD LOVES YOU deeply. His Word is filled with promises that reveal His desire to bring healing, hope, and abundant life to every area of your being—body, mind, and spirit. More than anything, He wants a personal relationship with you through His Son, Jesus Christ.

If you've never invited Jesus into your life, you can do so right now. It's not about religion—it's about a relationship with the One who knows you completely and loves you unconditionally. If you're ready to take that step, simply pray this prayer with a sincere heart:

> *Lord Jesus, I want to know You as my Savior and Lord. I confess and believe that You are the Son of God and that You died for my sins. I believe You rose from the dead and are alive today. Please forgive me for my sins. I invite You into my heart and my life. Make me new. Help me to walk with You, grow in Your love, and live for You every day. In Jesus' name, amen.*

If you just prayed that prayer, you've made the most important decision of your life. All of heaven rejoices with you, and so do I! You are now a child of God, and your journey with Him has just begun.

Please contact my publisher at pray4me@charismamedia.com so we can send you some materials that will help you become established in your relationship with the Lord. We look forward to hearing from you.

NOTES

CHAPTER 1

1. *Oxford English Dictionary*, "dysfunction," accessed April 24, 2025, https://www.oed.com/dictionary/dysfunction_n?tab=factsheet#5883226.
2. Joni and Friends, accessed April 24, 2025, https://joniandfriends.org.

CHAPTER 4

1. Vince Lombardi, "Leaders are made, they are not born. They are made by hard effort, which is the price which all of us must pay to achieve any goal that is worthwhile," Vince Lombardi Official Website, accessed April 24, 2025, https://vincelombardi.com/quotes/.
2. "Real leaders are ordinary people with extraordinary determination!," commonly attributed to an unknown author.

CHAPTER 5

1. Charles Haddon Spurgeon, "Patient Job, and the Baffled Enemy," sermon delivered August 28, 1890, The Spurgeon Center, accessed April 25, 2025, https://www.spurgeon.org/resource-library/sermons/patient-job-and-the-baffled-enemy/#flipbook/.

CHAPTER 8

1. James Strong, *The New Strong's Exhaustive Concordance of the Bible* (Thomas Nelson, 1995), "G4611."

Chapter 13

1. Bible Hub, "τυφλός *tuphlos*," accessed April 24, 2025, https://biblehub.com/greek/strongs_5185.htm.

Chapter 14

1. "Parasitism," WikiDoc, accessed April 24, 2025, https://www.wikidoc.org/index.php/Parasitism.

Chapter 16

1. Gerald Zaltman, "*The Subconscious Mind of the Consumer (and How to Reach It)*," Harvard Business School, accessed April 24, 2025, https://www.library.hbs.edu/working-knowledge/the-subconscious-mind-of-the-consumer-and-how-to-reach-it.

Chapter 18

1. Charles Stanley, "God's Pathway of Brokenness," In Touch Ministries, accessed April 24, 2025, https://www.intouch.org/watch/sermons/life-principle-15-gods-pathway-of-brokenness.

Chapter 19

1. Bible Hub, "*skandalon*," accessed April 24, 2025, https://biblehub.com/greek/4625.htm.
2. Dr. Caroline Leaf, *Who Switched Off My Brain?* (Thomas Nelson, 2009).
3. Bible Hub, "*chairó*," accessed April 24, 2025, https://biblehub.com/greek/5463.htm.

ACKNOWLEDGMENTS

FIRST, TO MY precious wife, Cristina—you are the one who sat, stood, laughed, and cried with me every minute of every hour of every day I wrote this book. I literally could not have done any of this without you. Your support, love, and wisdom have been poured into me and can be felt in the words of this book. You are the most amazing wife. You are a phenomenal mother and an exceptional pastor, preacher, and leader. I am so honored to call you my wife.

To my parents—Dad, I have seen your faults and failures. I've seen you at your lowest points in life. I've seen you broken. I've seen you hopeless. But I've also seen you become the man of God I most admire and model my life after. You have taken responsibility for your life. You have made freedom, healing, and character the paramount standard for your life; thus, it has become that for our family. Without your mess, I never would've been able to experience the miracle of this book. Thank you for the years of impartation, teaching, and knowledge you have passed down. I am forever grateful.

Mom, you are literally one of the strongest people I have ever known. Your grit, tenacity, and inability to give up never cease to amaze me. Believe me, it has made me who I am today. Thank you for the countless hours you spent helping us edit, organize, and rearrange the content of this book. Thank you for all the advice and wisdom you've added to this entire project.

To BJ Broome—simply put, I cannot imagine doing this project without your involvement. Your administrative, literary, and organizational input has added great value to this book. I'm thankful for your excitement, efficiency, and excellence. And as always, you have been nothing but a joy to work with.